Those Who Passed By

Eleanor Turnbull

 Light Messages

Durham, NC

Those Who Passed By
Eleanor Turnbull
Edited by Laura Brown
lightmessages.com/eleanor-turnbull
eturnbull@lightmessages.com

Published 2017, by Light Messages
www.lightmessages.com
Durham, NC 27713 USA
SAN: 920-9298

Paperback ISBN: 978-1-61153-236-4
Ebook ISBN: 978-1-61153-237-1
Library of Congress Control Number: 2017908194

To those who passed by,
to those who stayed,
and to those who served

The House by the Side of the Road

There are hermit
souls that live withdrawn
In the peace of their self-content;
There are souls, like stars, that dwell apart,
In a fellowless firmament;
There are pioneer souls that blaze their paths
Where highways never ran;
But let me live by the side of the road
And be a friend to man.

Let me live in a house
by the side of the road,
Where the race of men go by—
The men who are good and the men who are bad,
As good and as bad as I.
I would not sit in the scorner's seat,
Or hurl the cynic's ban;
Let me live in a house by the side of the road
And be a friend to man.

I see from my house
by the side of the road,
By the side of the highway of life,
The men who press with the ardor of hope,
The men who are faint with the strife.
But I turn not away from their smiles nor their tears
Both parts of an infinite plan;
Let me live in my house by the side of the road
And be a friend to man.

I know there are brook-gladdened
meadows ahead
And mountains of wearisome height;
That the road passes on through the long afternoon
And stretches away to the night.
But still I rejoice when the travelers rejoice,
And weep with the strangers that moan,
Nor live in my house by the side of the road
Like a man who dwells alone.

Let me live in my
house by the side of the road
Where the race of men go by—
They are good, they are bad, they are weak, they are strong,
Wise, foolish—so am I.
Then why should I sit in the scorner's seat
Or hurl the cynic's ban?
Let me live in my house by the side of the road
And be a friend to man.

Sam Walter Foss

PREFACE

I lift up my eyes toward the mountains—
from where will my help come?
My help is from the Lord,
maker of heaven and earth.

Psalm 121

A s the plane descended through the clouds, the U-shaped bay of Haiti unfolded before me like a stage. A scene of tranquility met my eyes as the clouds lifted and I saw the small boats sailing in the harbor of Port-au-Prince, tiny against the looming backdrop of high mountains. Only as the light became brighter could I see that the boats' sails were torn and patched and that the heavy, awkward, hand-made cargo vessels were over-loaded with sacks of charcoal, sea salt, and passengers. The smaller *boombas*, hand-made canoes from hollowed-out trees, carried a single fisherman using throw nets and Z-shaped bamboo fish traps to raid the waters of its already fast-diminishing life.

When I stepped onto the Haitian stage, I stepped around half-room-size piles of rotting garbage, crowded shanties, street beggars, and vertical layers of bustling human life, all telling the story of the intense struggle to survive. My senses were overwhelmed by the smells and sounds: roaring diesel trucks, constant horn blowing, and jackhammers taking out the last chunks of broken cement on Main Street.

Through all of this—and maybe because of it—I kept looking upward and towards the backdrop. Just to the right was a white limestone cliff reaching into the blue tropical sky. I had to tilt my head backward to find the top of the immediate mountains and then tilt even further backward to see the more distant ranges. This backdrop gave reality to the often-repeated proverb, *deye mon gen mon*. Behind mountains there are mountains.

I immediately felt overwhelmed. I was twenty-three years old with a Master's Degree in Christian Education, and until that day in 1947, I'd had no exposure to the extreme poverty found in the developing world. God had chosen Haiti as my mother's mission field, and I was there to check in on her before embarking on the mission I thought God had for me: flying bush planes in Africa. As I walked, I thought, "The situation here is too much. There is so much to be done. Where does one begin? How does one begin?"

When my eyes saw the little metal sign ROUTE KENSCOFF, I did not realize God was answering my question. I was not looking for my husband, my life, nor my ministry, but God would have me find them all.

That first day as I traveled in a *tap-tap* on the Kenscoff Road, it was a slippery, muddy mess of clay. Red, dirty water went rushing downhill, carrying rocks and trash in its turbulent flow. We passed masses of people moving in and out. A large group of bare-footed women carrying heavy loads on their heads gathered under an over-hanging cliff, and I heard them chattering in Creole as they readjusted their heavy loads of fifty to eighty-pound baskets with a few live chickens tied to the outside. Through my open window, I also heard a shrill Morse-code-like trumpeting I later learned was the sound of a conch-shell horn announcing community news across the mountains.

Taking in the natural beauty and awesome scenery, I was mystified. There was a feeling of isolation intensified by a language understood only by nationals, and a rural, sometimes impassable, countryside; yet the people expressed such a warmth in their boisterous expression of social happiness and obvious pride, my soul reached out to them.

The Kenscoff Road was the way that these people, the mountain population, those considered "inside" and isolated, traveled to the "outside." The life of the "inside" people was busy with carrying water from whatever source was available for the family's use; foraging bits of sticks and stalks for cooking; eking out an existence from eroded, steep mountain plots; gathering *Pois Congo* beans; or pounding grain with a giant-size mortar and pestle. "Outside" was the mountain people's term for far enough out of the mountains to see metal-roofed houses, vehicles (jeeps and trucks) and people of lighter color. The road was being built under the supervision of the United States Army Corps of Engineers. Already, the "outside" was reaching the "inside" of Haiti, and soon the hope, for my mother, and later for myself, was that the road might be a means for the Haitian people to encounter the Light of Christ and be transformed forever.

On that warm day when I arrived, Mission staff was only my mother and a twenty-two-year-old young man named Wallace Turnbull. It soon became apparent that I was one of "those who passed by" and had been "sent" to the Mission because shortly thereafter Wallace and I were married. I stayed at the Mission on the Kenscoff Road for seventy years. I was so sure the plans I had for my life were God's plans, but in reality, my life was God's business, and I had to get out of the way.

I went to Haiti in obedience to God, knowing that my work would be in one way or another with the Haitian people, that through my life, they might see the hope that comes from Jesus. I didn't know about those who would pass by, those people whose lives would touch and change mine and the ones whose lives would be changed.

Those who passed by the Mission came for a variety of reasons. Some came to experience another culture and people. For some, it was to see the poor people, sort of like looking at animals in a zoo. For others, it was out of doubt and skepticism that people could be that bad off. Others came with international organizations. Some sought adventure or spiritual pursuits.

Some even came to do research for novels, term papers in sociology, history, and yes (in the poorest country in the Western world) in economics, language research, comparative religion, and more. One of the most studied religions was Vodou, the idea of zombies, possession, and all the spectacular. One famous opera student from England was researching to see if a common denominator existed between the ecstasy-induced fainting many youths experienced during the music of the Beatles, the passing out of the extremists of the charismatic movement, and Haitian Vodou possession.

Young people gave up their summer vacation time, delayed marriage, borrowed money to meet expenses to go and help, to serve, in Haiti at the Mission on the Kenscoff Road. More than a few visitors came seeking relief from the guilt of being from an affluent society, while others wisely wanted to widen their worldview.

These are their stories.

I came that they may have life and have it abundantly.

John 10:10

ON THE SIDE OF THE ROAD

The Mission's outreach was to all those "on the side of the road." That statement was often taken literally, and I remember one day in particular. The Kenscoff Road climbs to almost 5,000 feet over a distance of fourteen miles. It is hairy, with sharp bends, drop-offs of five hundred feet, and no guard rails. The first half of the distance is harrowingly dangerous with ceaseless big Mack dump trucks creeping down the steep mountains when loaded with marlstone from the LaBoule sand mines and tearing up the mountains when empty. Brake failures often caused tragedies when vehicles went over-the-edge or flipped upside-down. There was no bypass or second route, so all vehicles had to pass by the police station corner in Petionville. Although hitchhikers often waited at the corner, it was unusual to see a foreigner doing so. When I saw a foreign young man standing alone wishing for a ride up the hill, I decided to pick him up and was glad to find that he spoke some English.

He was a teacher from Aruba, Dutch by birth, who was on an adventure vacation alone in Haiti. He spoke no Creole or French, but in broken English, he told me he thought it might be interesting to visit the mountain town of Kenscoff. When I asked if he knew about the Mission, he said, no, he knew nothing about the Mission on the Kenscoff Road so had not planned to pass by.

During the forty minute drive up the mountain, we felt acquainted and laughed that he was being "taken" to the Mission. We shared about differences in educational systems, the Mission's commitment and involvement in Haiti, and I encouraged him to include spiritual pursuits in his vacation adventure and invited him to stay with us. He agreed and seemed to enjoy his visit. When he left to continue to the village of Kenscoff, he kindly thanked us and said in his Dutch accent, "Maybe ve can elp children in Haiti go to school. I try."

Undecided, I wondered if I had simply picked up a hitchhiker and "taken" him to the Mission or if there was something more. Some months later correspondence from the church of Bilderdijksstraat, Aruba brought the good news that the young man I had met would sponsor the education of five Haitian children. It was then we knew that the young hitchhiker had not been "taken" to the Mission but had been sent.

Those first five sponsored children in Haiti have long since finished their six years of primary school. They were part of the generation that cried. They cried for more: more opportunity, more choices, more hope, and more education. Their cries resulted in our beginning the first secondary school in the mountains. These young Haitians became part of what might be termed "the exploding generation."

I remember once when I was at a conference, a gentleman commented, "The rural peasants are a developing society." A young Haitian doctor spoke up to say, "They cannot 'develop.' This is the emerging time." And so it was. Over the years where once only an occasional parent would allow his son to attend simple literacy centers, there grew a full fundamental education program to grade three. This "emerging" process became a "development" process as the students moved onward to a full primary school through grade six. With about forty percent becoming literate, where once literacy among the population was in the single digits, it then exploded to fifty percent of the population under the age of eighteen being able to read.

I do not know if the nice hitchhiker I picked up in Petionville near the ROUTE KENSCOFF sign and "TOOK" to the Mission is still teaching in Aruba. I do know that because he had been sent, several hundred—five at a time—economically disfavored children in Haiti received a primary education. Many of them are now part of that "exploding society." These children remind us of the Haitian proverb that "little as it may be, dried cod is meat." The little guy is somebody, too, and "little is much when God is in it."

He Maketh No Mistake

My Father's way may twist and turn
My heart may throb and ache,
But in my soul I'm glad to know,
He maketh no mistake.

My cherished plans may go astray,
My hopes may fade away,
But still I'll trust my Lord to lead,
For He doth know the way.

Tho' night be dark and it may seem
That day will never break,
I'll pin my faith, my all, in Him,
He maketh no mistake.

There's so much now I cannot see,
My eyesight's far too dim,
But come what may,
I'll simply trust and leave it all to Him.

For by and by the mist will lift,
And plain it all He'll make,
Through all the way, tho' dark to me,
He made not one mistake.

A. M. Overton

TWO WALLACES

It was so long ago I might forget about when Henry Wallace visited us, except for a photocopy of his check for $25.00, which we kept as a souvenir. He came without fanfare and even without introduction. Without knowing that he was a former vice-president of the United States, I received him in what, at that time, was our home.

Our house started as just one room made with chunks of limestone dug out from the mountainside, a rough cement floor; undressed native wood poles and reused corrugated metal sheets formed the roof. It had a heavy flap door made from planks, and window shutters were made from grocery store crates. It would have been nice to have some sort of ceiling to keep the scorpions, lizards, and even rats, harbored by the bark on the native poles, from falling down on us. They were primarily active at night, and that is when it took so long to find a match and light the lamp. There was no need for electrical wiring as there was no electricity. No plumbing installation was necessary as the toilet was a deep hole with slats providing semi-privacy. Water was available, with restrictions, when rain run-off was gathered from the corrugated roof. We are now ashamed to admit that we were part of the final demise of Haiti's few trees as we and many others used charcoal made from them to cook on the one-pot brazier.

Perhaps the name froze my brain as he introduced himself as "Mr. Henry Wallace." All I could think of was my husband Wallace, who was away for the day. Mr. Wallace mentioned that he hoped to return the next day to meet my husband, known to locals as Pastor Wallace. He spoke about the importance of agriculture in a country where eighty percent of the population was rural, and production was regressing, resulting in widespread hunger, high infant mortality, and extreme malnutrition among young children. As he mentioned leaving, I shared a quick word with him about my personal Christian faith and purpose in being a missionary in the steep over-populated mountain area—an area where land misuse and erosion gave reason for the farmers to say "the land is tired," and like their children, "the mountains are showing their bones."

Mr. Wallace did not stay long, and upon leaving, he politely asked if it would be "permitted for him to make a little donation." I assured him that it would, and he wrote his check.

My Wallace returned home that evening and was much more aware of who Henry Wallace was than I had been. He made me understand that Mr. Wallace had been Vice-President of the United States, Secretary of Agriculture, and had notable influence in high places. Though badly in need of the donation, I asked if perhaps we should keep the check as a souvenir instead of cashing it. Wallace's wise and practical response was, "Photocopy it." So, the next time we were in Port-au-Prince, we did both.

When Henry Wallace returned the next day, he and Pastor Wallace had a talk. My Wallace had wanted to find a more constructive way to use surplus food from the United States than simply handing it out in bits and pieces to crowds of people. Their conversation led to a new approach of using the surplus to help thousands of families in Haiti, as well as other countries, in what became known as Food for Work programs. In 1954 Hurricane Hazel blasted soil, the remaining trees, vegetation, and life off the mountains of Western Haiti. The American government responded with quantities of life-saving bulk foods.

Eventually, the conversation between the two Wallaces turned into plan PL480 passed by US Congress. For more than 40 years, shiploads of relief would be sent to Haiti and other countries to be used as payment for work done in times of crisis. Because of this, a pattern of discipline and integrity like that of which Mr. Henry Wallace and my husband Wallace had dreamed about and discussed together was realized.

As one "who passed by" the Mission on the Kenscoff Road, Mr. Wallace left much more than a check for $25.00.

Disappointment

"Disappointment—His Appointment"
"No good thing will He withhold,"
From denials oft we gather
Treasures of His love untold,
Well He knows each broken purpose
Leads to fuller, deeper trust,
And the end of all His dealings
Proves our God is wise and just.

"Disappointment—His Appointment"
Lord, I take it, then, as such.
Like the clay in hands of potter,
Yielding wholly to Thy touch.
All my life's plan in Thy moulding,
Not one single choice be mine;
Let me answer, unrepining—
"Father, not my will, but Thine."

Edith Lillian Young

FI YO

Before the Mission on the Kenscoff Road became a destination and the region was just called the "Fort Jacques area" and the "Western section," two young Ivy League graduates volunteered with the Friends Service Committee to go to Haiti. Bobbi had graduated from Dartmouth and Polly from Swarthmore. With little instruction, less local language ability, and no provision of the simplest equipment, the team leader helped them find a local residence—a mud-plastered hut with a thatch roof. The nearest water supply was one hour away across another mountain. With no personal privacy and no kitchen, the ladies were given the daunting task to get to know the people of the community and help them.

As you may imagine, the Haitians were intrigued by the women's presence. They wondered, *Why are they here? What is their purpose?* They soon discovered the ladies' names were Bobbi and Polly, but among themselves, the Haitians called them *fi yo*, "the girls."

With the exception of Wallace and me, fi yo were the only other non-Haitians living in the Western area. We decided we needed to get acquainted with fi yo and encouraged them to learn the local Creole language. Once a week we invited them to come to the Mission to get a shower and then listened as they shared how things were going. We were trying to discover their purpose as much as the locals. Fi yo were a stark contrast to the Haitians they were serving—Bobbi and Polly were educated but did not have many life skills, while ninety-five percent of the Haitian population was illiterate but had learned hard life lessons.

Oh, the stories Bobbi and Polly would tell! Polly loved constellations. It was impressive to listen to her talk about her teaching. She would sit outside looking up into the night sky with her back arched. Without light, chalk, a pencil, or a book, she pointed out the place and name of every constellation in that marvelous sky. Then there was the mix-up when Bobbi wanted something different for breakfast instead of the usual cornmeal mush. She consulted her Creole/English vocabulary booklet and thought she had learned the word for eggplant to go along with some eggs. Unfortunately, she confused the Creole word *bètrav* with the word *berijen*. Greatly disappointed, Bobbi complained that any vegetable would have been better. She did not really enjoy her boiled beets and eggs for breakfast.

One day the women discovered that forty-five-gourde notes, about the equivalent of twenty U.S. dollars, were missing from their home. Who stole the money? Many of the local people believed in the power of Vodou and called on the *houngan* (witchdoctor) to perform the "trial." With a group of several suspects, the case was processed as Janwa, the houngan, sat the suspects in a little low chair one at time and attempted to raise it with bunches of pigeon pea branches held in each hand. If the little chair was lifted by the twigs, the person sitting in the chair was guilty. If the weight of the chair pulled the chair down through the little branches, the suspect was announced innocent and freed. One poor suspect was found guilty, his chair rising in the air. Polly and Bobbie were horrified when he was taken into custody. But the unorthodox trial did work out for those involved.

We took an angry Polly to the village police where she was able to get the incarcerated man released. And when fi yo arrived back at their little mud hut, a packet of forty-five bright, new gourde notes had been laid in front of the hut's door.

Eventually, unrest in Haiti under the presidency of Papa Doc and his Tonton Macouts, made the Friends USA office close their Haiti branch and return Bobbi and Polly to the States. Before they left, fi yo talked with their community leader Pastor Eloizil about what purpose he could see in their leaving. Having learned so much of the culture and habits of the people, and having formed friendships within the warm, embracing Kenscoff Road communities, Bobbi and Polly analyzed the questions: What had they accomplished? Why should they leave, and with what purpose?

Pastor Eloizil believed fi yo would play a critical role in building a community school with Christian principles for the Haitian people. Bobbi and Polly could return to Boston to await legalization of a site for the school, meanwhile designing floor plans, training teachers, and overseeing the project as needed. The ladies agreed to the plan and returned to the United States.

Many of Haiti's upward-moving citizens are grateful for the primary school in Fort Jacques started by Bobbi and Polly. Yet not many Haitians remember the school's founders. When questioned, a person will answer, "Who? When?" and rarely someone will respond, "Oh, you mean fi yo?" Yet even if people don't remember Bobbi and Polly by name, many experience the positive results of their lives—improved literacy in Haiti, education for children, and for some, a reconciled relationship with God. Jesus said, "I have come that they may have life, and that they may have it more abundantly" (John 10:10). God surely sent fi yo to Haiti, and we were privileged to have a small glimpse of how He used them to enrich the lives of others and fulfill His divine purpose in a little school off the Kenscoff Road.

Whatever you do, work heartily, as for the Lord and not for men, knowing that from the Lord you will receive the inheritance as your reward. You are serving the Lord Christ.

Colossians 3:23-24

HEALING HOOCH

Another donation to the Mission had more high-spirited results. Barbancourt Rum is now famous in Haiti, and when we first met Rudolph, he had recently met and married the former "Miss Haiti" of the Barbancourt family. Most of Jane's family property had been destroyed at the time of the 1804 War for Independence, but she still had the recipe for the famous Barbancourt Rum as well as the ruins of old distilleries on what remained of her family's run-down land.

When Jane met Rudolph, she was not interested in developing her heritage. Perhaps it had seemed too large a task. But with her husband by her side, she put parts of the old lands back into business by enlarging the distillery and creating a sampling room as a tourist attraction. It was a beautiful castle-style stone complex where they proudly boasted one hundred and ten flavors of rum: coffee, coconut, banana, hibiscus, ginger, etc. There were chandeliers of brown rum bottles, an old cane mill with wooden rollers, and a mock distillery with antique copper stills. It was a favorite place for foreign tourists to visit and was off the Kenscoff Road before the turn to the Mission.

We had always been friendly with Rudolph and Jane, but after their two sons had shown interest in a children's Bible club at the Mission, we made time to see them more often. One year, a few days before Christmas, I was going to Port-au-Prince, so I stopped by to wish them a Merry Christmas and give them a gift of a special Christmas bread from the Mission. Rudolph, warmly touched by the gesture from the Mission, reached on the shelf behind him and took down two bottles of his special rum. As he put them in a straw in a shopping bag, I protested, "Thank you Rudolph, but you know that we do not drink rum."

He gently said, "Yes, I know that, but this is Christmas," as he put in two more bottles! Again protesting, I said, "Please don't— it is not at all necessary since we do not drink at the Mission at Christmas either."

As he insisted and handed me the basket with the four bottles of rum, he gently said, "You don't drink, but you can use it for cooking, so I will give you these recipes," and he slipped a brochure of Barbancourt recipes in the bag. There was nothing for me to do but wish him a blessed and meaningful Christmas for himself and his family and leave.

That evening I folded the straw shopping bag with the four bottles of rum down tightly and put it far behind the Christmas tree which already had some gifts in bright wrapping paper and ribbons. We had established a tradition at the Mission of an early Christmas morning with our family. Then later, a group of about thirty to forty of the most neglected and alone, several of them blind, crippled, and elderly, would gather for a reading of the Christmas story and sing Christmas carols translated into the Creole language. They would pray together, open gifts, and close with a piece of cake and Haitian cola (an extra-sweet, perfume-tasting soda).

On Christmas morning, after the family gifts had been given and appreciated, Wallace pulled out the straw bag, commenting, "What is this?"

He took out the first bottle, which promptly slid through the roll of soft cardboard protecting it and hit the cement floor, shattering glass and flooding the place with rum.

Never wanting to waste anything, I shouted, "Get a pan—save it! Catch the alcohol—it can be used at the clinic!"

We rushed around to save the last bit of rum from the broken bottle, but our greatest concern quickly became, "How are we going to get the fumes out of the house before the Christmas morning group arrives? What will the people think?"

Our response was quick. We opened all the windows, grabbed the bleach, and scrubbed. We did everything and anything to kill the smell of Barbancourt Rum all through the Mission house that Christmas morning!

Lord, Help me Live from Day to Day

Lord, let me live from day to day,
In such a self-forgetful way,
That even when I kneel to pray,
My pray'r shall be for *others*.

Help me in all the work I do
To ever be sincere and true,
And know that all I'd do for you
Must needs be done for *others*.

Let "Self" be crucified and slain
And buried deep, nor rise again
And may all efforts be in vain,
Unless they be for *others*.

So when my work on earth is done,
And my new work in heav'n's begun,
May I forget the crown I've won,
While thinking still of *others*.

Yes, others, Lord, yes, others,
Let this my motto be;
Help me to live for others,
That I may live like Thee.

Charles D. Meigs

CAMOUFLAGED GIFT

There was so much criticism of foreign missionaries out there that I often worried about what others thought, and I strived to be a positive example to the foreigners as well as to the Haitians. I learned that when anything good came from obeying God, misunderstandings were bound to happen from time to time. One misunderstanding nearly cost me my life, and it all began when I met Earl and Marion.

It was a typical, bright, sunny Sunday morning in the high hills of Haiti. I was rushing up the steep grade of our campus driveway to get our toddler to his Creole Sunday School class. Traffic was rare in those days when the road was only partially complete, so I was startled and impressed when a fine, black government sedan pulled into the Mission and stopped. The Haitian driver was our old friend Pastor Arthur, Haitian ambassador to Washington, and he introduced me to Earl and his wife, Marion. Hosted by President Eugene Magloire of Haiti, Earl was on his second visit inspecting a housing project contracted by his engineering company in Moline, Illinois. Pastor Arthur explained that the couple had requested to visit a Christian mission. Earl was impressed by the beauty of Haiti as well as the poverty and the gentle, friendly people. He knew his wife would want to take as much information as possible back to their Methodist church's missions' committee. I see now that surely this couple had been sent to the Mission, as this meeting led to years of collaborating to bring economic benefits to the Haitian people when government efforts failed.

Earl used his international connections to bring leftover materials from projects he was involved with to Haiti. One such instance was when the United States was ridding their warehouses of unused and unwanted military clothing. Earl found ways for the United States Navy to transport the clothing to Port-au-Prince. Many bales were neckties, dress uniforms of wool or cotton, and camouflage uniforms: black, khaki, drab green, white, and blue in every size, shape, and kind.

The Mission on the Kenscoff Road had started Work-for-Clothes Projects for the poor mountain farmers of Haiti. The people hand-dug roads, improved foot trails, washed-out terraced gullies in mountainside areas, and quarried mountainside sites to build schools. A day's labor earned a shirt or a dress, two days' labor earned a pair of pants, and so it went. The people were glad for the clothes, and we found more opportunities to be a part of the community. The clothes Earl sent were used for these projects. There is still a joke today about the "mama pants" as the clothes were made to fit two-hundred-pound American soldiers, so they looked baggy on the thin Haitians. In Sunday morning church I would see women's skirts made of neckties, the men in double-breasted, gold-buttoned dress coats, and even camouflage jumpsuits.

One shipment of clothes, in particular, was stored in a warehouse in Port-au-Prince. We were unable to use open transport trucks to move the clothes to the Mission, so we decided that each time someone drove the station wagon into town to run errands, she'd load three bales of clothes in it from the warehouse and thus have enough clothing to keep the work projects going.

I was often the one to do those general errands which meant a hectic day of diverse activities and contacts. On this particular day, I remember one of the items I needed was sulfur powder. In those days, lack of hygiene spread scabies to households and school children, and for the general public, the cost of pharmacy treatment was not possible. Sulfur powder mixed into cooking lard or Vaseline made an effective, affordable treatment.

After shopping, I went to the warehouse and hurriedly loaded as much of the military clothing into the station wagon as space allowed. With half a ton of surplus U.S. military uniforms, five pounds of sulfur powder, food supplies, and a briefcase full of important Mission and customs documents, I was pressing up the Delmas highway toward Petionville, anticipating getting home to the Mission.

Suddenly, a car with darkened windows carrying four militiamen, known internationally as *Tonton Macouts*, motioned me over. Under Haiti's dictator, Papa Doc Duvalier, the Tonton Macouts enforced Duvalier's rules and later their own with force and brutality. So much so that the Haitians called them the Boogey Men, scaring their children with the mere mention of their name. In the 1960s, there was a tension between Washington and Papa Doc Duvalier, and he became nervous about the United States military clothing being used by anti-government guerrillas. Now the Tonton Macouts had my vehicle, filled with military clothing, surrounded and were interrogating me:

"What are you carrying?"

"Used clothing."

"What are you going to do with it?"

"Give it to the poor people in the mountains."

I quickly identified myself as I thought that telling them I was from the Mission and explaining that the clothes were a donation would help. However, one armed man roughly got into the station wagon, while the other shouted for me to turn around and follow them back toward Port-au-Prince. Meanwhile, the man in the vehicle took the packages and briefcase off the seat to make more room for himself. As I turned the station wagon around, he noticed some yellow powder sift out of a five-pound paper bag. It was at that moment that I remembered that guerrillas use sulfur powder mixed with charcoal to make gun powder.

Wiping his finger and smelling the powder the man asked, "What is this?"

I started to pray silently and answered, "That is sulfur powder used at the Mission clinic for an ointment for scabies." I then explained to him what scabies was. I described how children scratch, causing infection, and how the microscopic parasite causes itching as it moves and burrows beneath the skin.

He responded by saying, "Drive faster."

At the end of the Delmas Road, there is a fork in the road. To the left, was Port-au-Prince and the palace of the president. To the right was Fort National where unmentionable tortures were often reported. Shortly before this, the report was that the female leader of the Tonton Macoutes had ordered gasoline poured over her husband's alleged mistress' head and had her burned to death.

We turned left.

When we arrived at the palace, a guard opened the iron gate at the palace yard and motioned to where we should park. Locking the station wagon, I followed the armed men towards the palace entrance. Across the yard a man whose name I did not know cried out, "Madame Wallace, what are you doing here?"

"I don't know!" I replied. "Ask these armed guards!"

The man chose to walk on and left me with the guards. They took me to a quiet upstairs office where I was told to sit down and wait quietly until their chief came. They took my briefcase and left.

It was a long two hours with no way to contact the Mission, or anyone outside, and let them know my whereabouts. With plenty of time to gather my wits, reflect on my situation, and pray for strength, I eventually told the guards stationed at the door that it was important for me to get to the Mission. "Please, would you find the chief and ask him to see me?"

"He is with President Duvalier."

"Please tell President Duvalier that I need to leave."

Time passed. Eventually, a messenger came from the inner office with a message from the president.

"President Duvalier says we may let you go. However, you must tell your husband to be careful not to give too many military clothes in any one area in the countryside, and if possible, stain it another color.

"Yes, of course. Thank you. Would it be possible for one of the officers to escort me to the station wagon to assure the others of my permission to leave?" My request was granted, and I silently said a prayer of thanks to God for my deliverance and provision.

Far more than my freedom had been granted that day. In giving his directive, the President had in fact given us the right to claim all the clothes in the warehouse without question and have them all transported to the Mission. Genesis 50:20 came to mind as I drove back to the Mission, "But as for you, you meant evil against me; but God meant it for good, in order to bring it about as it is this day, to save many people alive."

—

The Winds of Fate

One ship drives east and another drives west
With the selfsame winds that blow.
'Tis the set of the sails
And not the gales
Which tells us the way to go.
Like the winds of the seas are the ways of fate,
As we voyage along through the life:
'Tis the set of a soul
That decides its goal,
And not the calm or the strife.

Ella Wheeler Wilcox

JANNWA

There was definitely darkness present when I arrived in Haiti. Most Haitians practiced Vodou, and witchdoctors made a living appeasing evil spirits, observing animalism, and guarding the family's sacred artifacts called fetishes for ceremonies where it was said the dead were raised as zombies, and family spirits, called *loas*, took possession of dancing participants. The *houngan*, or witchdoctor, lived in his peristyle hut and practiced his calling that passed from generation to generation. Little flags on a high pole marked an *houngan's* peristyle. Jannwa was an *houngan* and one of our closest neighbors on the Kenscoff Road.

Jesus said, "You shall love your neighbor as yourself," so we were good neighbors to Jannwa, and he felt comfortable enough to visit us at the Mission. We had such lively debates! I remember one visit where he told me, "I'm like you, Madame Wallace; I help the community." I was taken aback by the comment knowing that he practiced sorcery, so I objected, "No. Cursing and hexing people is not helping them." Jannwa was very sincere when he replied, "Oh, yes it is. I only curse the bad ones!"

Jannwa had a thriving business. Those passing by on the Kenscoff Road stopped to receive deliverance from poverty, distress, sickness, or fear, to appease the dead, for good luck, for a plentiful harvest, to obtain a visa for travel, to conceive, win the lottery, to find the perfect spouse. The list went on and on. We, and other Christians, often made clear to him the same message given to Nicodemus who went to inquire of Jesus, who answered him, "You must be born again" (John 3:7).

The day finally came when Jannwa sent a note that read, "You had your day at the fetish bonfires. I had my day when at ritual ceremonies I tied more sacred power knots in my Satan rope expecting that as the Vodou temple would be enriched so my son would be pleased and become the next *houngan*. TODAY IS GOD'S DAY. Can you come to pray with all my family and me? Please clean out the *hounfor* and leave nothing—not even the nails in the wall. Leave NOTHING. It is to be erased so that my son can never restore it. Just as Jesus has cleaned me and has erased all my past, so Satan worship must be erased from my family."

Hallelujah!

Jannwa is now dead, but I know his spirit is with Jesus. The last time I passed by I stopped by Jannwa's old place to reflect and rejoice. As Jesus said, "For God did not send His Son into the world to condemn the world, but that the world through Him might be saved" (John 3:17). And Jannwa was not the only *houngan* saved. Dormistoi, Nicolas, and Meristain were converts who felt the need to travel to the heights of Haiti—or "mountains" in Arawak, which indeed is what Haiti means—going about *travay Bon Dieu*, "the Good God's business." They had recently learned A.B. Simpson's missionary song, "To the regions beyond I must go, where the story has never been told." And so they went on foot over the long foot trails in the mountains visiting families and sharing the Good News.

These three men, who reminded me of the wise men of the traditional Christmas story, did not think of the dangers or self-deprivation involved in going out. With two gourdes in their pockets (forty cents) they would buy the hard bread and *rapadou* candy they would need to last them for the next several days.

Many times as they shared the Good News in the villages, their message was accepted, and new Christians would want their Vodou fetishes, ritual objects, and sacred items of trust and confidence to be burned on site. Other times, the tireless evangelists chose to return to the Mission on the Kenscoff Road with some items, appoint a time when new converts would gather with the local Christian community, and have a bonfire. As the news of fetish burning got around, nearby witchdoctors gathered to watch, verifying who of their former practitioners were now throwing costly fetishes into the fire. The church yard bonfires were a tradition my mother started and we continued. "For it is the God who commanded light to shine out of darkness, who has shone in our hearts to give the light of the knowledge of the glory of God in the face of Jesus Christ" (2 Corinthians 4:6).

The Weaver

My life is but a weaving betwixt the Lord and me,
I do not choose the color, He worketh steadily.
Oftimes He weaveth sorrow and I in foolish pride,
Forget He sees the upper, and I the underside.

Not till the loom is silent, and the shuttle cease to fly
Shall God unroll the canvas and explain the reason why.
The dark threads are as needful in the Weaver's skillful hand
As the threads of gold and silver in the pattern He has planned.

Grant Colfax Tullar

I KNOW A PLACE

A conversation about fetish bonfires, superstitions, and Vodou spirits opened the door for us to share the Gospel with a famous couple from the United States. The Mission was newly-established, and we were traveling with some of our first visitors, Dr. and Mrs. Sanders from Chicago, Illinois, who were celebrating their honeymoon. Mrs. Sanders was a social worker, and as we drove, she compared what she saw of Haiti's social conditions to what she experienced in Chicago.

We made a late-afternoon stop at Lorene's house to look in on her and her three children. Lorene always seemed to need help to feed her family who was unable to find water in which to bathe or wash clothing. Mrs. Sanders remarked that the lack of water, especially hot water, made it more difficult for me to care for the poor in Haiti. I agreed. As we were talking, I noticed Lorene's twelve-year-old daughter had pea-sized bumps all over her foot and lips caused by fleas' egg sacs buried under the skin. The condition was called *chic*, and the sacs had to be manually dug out, or they would fester. Without hesitation, I took a pin from my dress and got ready to work. However, I pierced the sac and had to duck as infected pus squirted out of the wound, almost hitting Mrs. Sanders who was startled and exclaimed, "I wouldn't know where to begin in a situation like this."

Mrs. Sanders was a good sport about everything though, and as we started the climb into the mountains on the Kenscoff Road, she commented on the busy crowds of people who packed the streets, and how despite impoverished conditions, were smiling and taking the time to talk to one another. She didn't seem to think about her discomfort at all during the bumpy, rough jeep ride back to the Mission along the steep, winding, narrow road.

Suddenly a little green Jeep pulled alongside us, and the foreign driver asked in English, "Is there some place up this way to get something to eat?"

Wallace and I quickly looked at each other with mutual understanding. The only "fast food" places were where local women squatted over charcoal braziers frying *marinad*, a dough patty made of flour, salt water, and maybe flakes of dried cod—definitely not a place a foreigner would feel comfortable buying food. We would have to take them to the Mission. Wallace replied, "We know a place! Follow us."

The green Jeep was close behind us as we pulled into the Mission and stopped in front of my mother's bungalow. I slipped into the kitchen and explained to Mom that we must make some tea and get ready to feed, if only with bread and butter, the hungry strangers we had invited to follow us home. While the water heated for tea, I noticed my mother, bless her heart, unselfishly preparing the only food fit for the company: a pack of American hot dogs she had been saving as her special birthday treat.

While Mom and I made preparations in the kitchen, Dr. and Mrs. Sanders were getting acquainted with the folks in the green Jeep, and Mrs. Sanders realized that she had attended a lecture given by the gentleman in Chicago.

Mrs. Sanders slipped into the kitchen and whispered, "Mrs. Wallace, perhaps you don't know, but your guests are famous. He is Leonard Bernstein, an American composer, and conductor. I attended a lecture he gave in Chicago last month. His wife was recently voted the best-dressed woman in America!"

I had no idea! We were isolated from American news and busy in the mountains of Haiti, so we did not know about Leonard Bernstein, but we did enjoy getting to know him and his wife over lunch. After holding hands while Wallace offered a prayer of thanks for the food, we all shared a simple meal served around an old-fashioned metal table in the kitchen lighted by a kerosene lamp.

There was ample conversation about family and questions and answers about Haiti. I was also quietly praying for an opportunity to share the Gospel with them. Talk of superstitions and Vodou spirits opened the door for my mother, known to everyone as Granny, to explain that although they are real, one need not be afraid of the Vodou spirits when the Holy Spirit, who is God's presence, is with him. God is ever-present with those who are saved and obey God' son, Jesus Christ.

There was a pause in the conversation at that point, and at length, Leonard said, "An opera is festering in my mind."

We all listened intently as he explained, "Imagine a stage covered in Spanish moss with colored lights creating areas of light and darkness. Prowling Vodou spirits would be maneuvering around the stage, always asking for appeasement and controlling the Earth's population by fear. All the while, high above all this would be the glory light of Jehovah-God who would be watching, seeing it all. In the end, the glory light would overcome the darkness, brighten the stage, and free the people from fear."

Mrs. Sanders, who had been listening intently, replied, "If you had been with us this afternoon, you would have seen real festering!" And she went on to explain with great drama our experience at Lorene's. We couldn't help but laugh.

It was late when the Bernsteins had to leave to make their way back into the city. As Mr. Bernstein left, he embraced us ladies. Holding Granny in his arms, he said, "You have been wonderful. We will never forget you."

He wrote us a lovely letter of thanks from Puerto Rico. Years later, I remember Granny would smile, her eyes twinkling as she told younger missionary women, "Don't be discouraged; I had to wait sixty-nine years to be held in the arms of a famous man."

Dr. Sanders later wrote to tell us that after attending one of Leonard Bernstein's famous concerts, the composer had received him backstage and shared how vividly the mission experience in Haiti had remained with him.

We asked God to send to the Mission those of His choosing, and because of this, we had to believe that those who passed by had truly been sent. Through the following years, as we would read of Leonard Bernstein's beautiful music and great success, we prayed that he might be among those who would find "the glory Light of Jehovah" and be released from fears of sin and self. Years later, when we read in *TIME* magazine that he had died, we felt that we had lost a friend.

Would You?

If you had been to heathen lands
Where weary souls stretch out their hands
To plead, yet no one understands
Would you help? Would you?

If you had seen the women bear
Their heavy loads with none to share
Had heard them weep with none to care
Would you help? Would you?

If you had seen the glorious sight
When heathen people in their night
Were brought from darkness into light
Would you help? Would you?

Yet still they wait, a weary throng
They've waited, some so very long
When shall despair be turned to song?
Will you help the weary throng?

Unknown

SUPERSTITIONS?

L eonard Bernstein was not the only famous man I did not recognize. When a filming team from England called to ask if I would meet with Cliff Richards and talk to him about children in Haiti, I had no idea who he was. It was only after he left that I realized he was the British pop star who had recently starred in the musical comedy *Summer Holiday*.

That first day when we met, I accidentally called him James instead of Cliff; he smiled and corrected me. He was there to make a film to raise global concern for the plight of children in Haiti and was genuinely enthusiastic about the future of those reached with the Gospel through Christian schools. We talked about many things, but one moment stands out as we were sitting in a cemetery and Cliff asked, "The mortality rate for children is so high in Haiti. Are children afraid of death?"

"Yes, of course. But Vodou practice only intensifies their fears."

"What do you mean?"

"Since in Vodou, spirits come back from the dead to haunt or capture the living, a daughter is taught to fear her deceased mother. There are superstitions they believe protect them."

"Superstitions?"

"Sometimes the living throw sesame seeds on the grave as they leave. The belief is that the zombie will then stop to count the seeds, will lose count because there are too many, and start over repeatedly, giving the living time to escape home. Food offerings are also left to appease the dead." I pointed to the altar with a tall cross in the middle of the cemetery. "And others believe they can pay Baron Samedi to curse and kill their enemies over something as small as an argument. People make requests with Baron Samedi at the altar, leaving pieces of fingernails, hair, a crudely made cloth doll, or a miniature coffin with the victim's name on a piece of paper inside it."

After talking with Cliff, I was certain that in his heart he had both an understanding and a commitment to the One who said, "Let the little children come to me... for such is the kingdom of heaven." I also knew that the gift of song and rhythm God had put in Cliff would be used to tell of Haiti's children scrounging in garbage heaps and dying without care. It did not take long to confirm this, for shortly after Cliff's visit, his organization found sponsors for hundreds of Haiti's children.

Forth into the darkness passing,
Nothing can I hear or see,
Save the Hand outstretched to guide me,
And the Voice that calls to me,
"I will bring the blind by pathways
That they knew not, nor have known;
"'Tis a way untried. untrodden,
But they shall not walk alone."

John Johnstone

TI KAY

When Hurricane Hazel hit Haiti on October 15, 1954, it became the measuring stick we used to compare the damage brought by every other storm we ever experienced at the Mission on the Kenscoff Road. We had no warning on our old-fashioned short-wave Philips radio before the hurricane. The local *tele-djòl*, word of mouth, casually mentioned that the winds and changing clouds indicated a *move tan*, bad time or bad weather, was coming. What an understatement! The Category 4 storm winds ripped off the heavy metal roofing sheets from our house and sent them flying like kites; the Berly side of the mountain split and avalanched downward, taking every homestead, person, and animal in its path, burying everything in its rumbling sliding glide.

It did not take an engineer to see that the houses made of woven sticks and mud-plastered walls set on shoveled-out sites were sitting ducks for runoff from mountain storms that seasonally collapsed them. Wallace and I looked at the devastation after Hazel and thought, "There must be a better way." Why not show the people how to put a home above the ground so runoff water could pass under it without demolishing it? We also thought how a house made from boards would be warmer in winter. Thus the idea for *Ti Kay*, the Little House, was born. Hurricane Hazel created plenty of building materials found in the blown-down, uprooted, oversized pine trees. Rolling the heavy logs to mountainside scaffolds of strong branches, an experienced sawyer and trained helper armed with only a seven-foot cross-cut saw, steel wedges, and a sledge hammer could turn the fallen trees into 2'x10' timbers. It was an amazing process to watch. Standing above the log, the carpenter, or *boss*, would push the long cross-cut saw down while his helper below immediately pushed it back up. The two of them became the lumber mill, spending many weeks making much-needed boards of various sizes and shapes. When the scaffolding gave way, and a log scooted downhill, the patient team jacked the log up on a new scaffold and continued. It was at the Mission on Kenscoff Road that the model little house, Ti Kay, with a wood floor and recycled aluminum roof was made from the Hurricane Hazel hand-sawn boards.

While Ti Kay on the Kenscoff Road had a unique beginning, over the years, many different kinds of people passed by and found refuge in the little house for the furtherance of God's Kingdom. As Samuel Foss wrote in his poem "The House By the Side of the Road":

> Let me live in my house by the side of the road,
> Where the race of men go by—
> They are good, they are bad, they are weak, they are
> strong,
> Wise, foolish—so am I.

Vonik, an architect's wife and talented artist, became a friend to the Mission and expressed an interest in helping in the community. Her opportunity came when we met Odes and Charles. Odes was the oldest of five orphaned children from the far Northwest of Haiti. He and his younger brother Charles were both artistic and wanted to paint pictures to sell. Vonik turned

Ti Kay into a studio where she taught the brothers and other budding artists how to use remnant denim fabric as canvases.

About that time the famous Issa El Saieh was known to have the place to find the best paintings at the best price. He chose wisely and facilitated the foremost painters of Haiti. Issa was a kind man, and fortunately for us, he was interested in the happenings at the Mission. We were able to introduce him to Odes and Charles and the other unknown, budding artists at Ti Kay. Issa promised, "We will do what we can for them!" Encouraged and guided by Vonik and Issa El Saieh the demand and value of the paintings of the Ti Kay artists' rose until they were well sought after and known.

Eventually, Odes was able to move to the city with his brother as their financial situation improved. Odes wanted to show his gratitude to his mountain friends, so he arrived at the Mission with a beautiful large painting as a gift. I thanked him for the gift but asked him to explain the meaning of the painting's subject: an angry-looking hen watching a bright plaid-covered snake stealing an egg from the hen's nest. Odes' explanation was, "The eggs are the children of the church from which the devil is stealing the next generation!" The tableau is now on display in the *Musée du Peuple* at the Mission. Both Odes and Charles lived out the story of the talents in Mathew 25:29: "For to everyone who has, more will be given, and he will have abundance."

Yolette was the next to find refuge in the little house. Before coming to the Mission, she had been home alone cooking a pot of cornmeal and dried beans for the family's next meal over a little wood fire. She suffered a violent seizure that threw her into the flames. Her family eventually found her there, and neighbors helped them tie her onto a stretcher of make-do poles and sticks. They carried her for five hours to the hospital at the Mission. There, the medical personnel uncovered the red, cooked flesh of a brave, suffering young woman expected to die.

Through days of cleaning, dressing, and caring, the medical folks realized that infection was causing decay. In addition to being at risk for infection from the other patients at the hospital, the stench and loud screaming during treatment were unnerving to all around. It was evident that Yolette needed a place apart, somewhere clean and private, where she could continue to receive necessary treatment. So Ti Kay became Yolette's healing ground and sanctuary for the next six months.

Every three to four days during that time, a member of Yolette's family would appear with pots of cooked food and washed garments. I can't imagine how the family and Yolette got through such a time, but the calendar showed that after six months Yolette started to walk and her family came with a "rented" horse to help her home. I think back to how she prayed and thanked God for his care and love and for the little house used to save her burned body as well as to learn the words to "Jesus Loves Me This I Know" in English, which were her parting words.

Ti Kay was already serving purposes beyond our understanding when one day a hired car and driver brought a woman we would always refer to as "Madame Lulu" to the Mission on the Kenscoff Road. Both her chauffeur and her secretary were staff that she had brought from New York and were English-speaking Haitians. Madame Lulu's secretary, Marie Denise, was a Christian and was so baffled by the woman's behavior that she brought her employer to the Mission in hopes we could help.

Before Marie Denise had an opportunity to talk with any of the Mission's staff, the strong, professional-like personality of Madame Lulu flooded us with information about herself—her extensive education and multiple degrees, her notoriety as a writer and impressive success as a consultant.

She told us she was in need of a place to stay where she could live "naturally." We offered her the guest apartment to which she exclaimed, "Oh no!" The painted walls would aggravate her extreme allergies. A bed would be "the death of her." We showed her Ti Kay with no electricity or plumbing. She loved it and offered to pay us something to stay there. We didn't need payment, so we agreed that in return for the lodgings she would to read the Gospel of John during her stay. We promptly found a dried banana bark straw mat for her to sleep on. Unable to stand smoke, she had Marie Denise put the charcoal brazier at a distance from Ti Kay and began to boil some whole red beets for her supper.

We did not know her real name. Our friend Cal, a former US Navy Chaplain and counselor, and his wife, Ginny, were involved with an English language ministry in the capital city. They came to the Mission often to visit us and enjoy the cool, clear air. It was Cal who gave her the name "Lulu" after spending time talking with her and trying to counsel her.

She told us she was a "sexologist"— a term we had never heard before. She very professionally explained that she counseled people about the importance of their sex lives. She boasted about her popularity as a "scientific writer for American magazines" and explained that she advised people about the importance of their sex lives and fantasies. It was only after she told details of her profession that her secretary found an opportunity to secretly tell us details and give us a copy of a sex magazine she published with articles she had written. We were horrified at such explicit, pornographic content and immediately burned it all.

Madame Lulu spoke of "being on medication" but was unable to give precise information about her doctor, her prescriptions, her diagnosis, or prognosis. She read the gospel of John and would briefly talk with Christians on campus. She continued to boil whole red beets over charcoal and scream at us with bitter accusations that the bits of smoke in the air from the hospital kitchen caused her unbalanced behavior. After three days she began walking around the Mission campus calling out to the trees.

She continued to scold and chastise us for our lack of concern for her well-being and in general became impossible. After trying to reason with her, Cal advised that it was time for Madame Lulu to leave the Mission. With Cal's help, we hired a car to take the only actively practicing sexologist we had ever known to the airport.

Some of us are still searching to understand why "Lulu, the Sexologist" passed by the Mission on the Kenscoff Road. Perhaps just experiencing God's love through others and reading the Gospel of John was purpose enough.

Recently, when I went to check on Ti Kay, it wasn't standing where it had always been. I asked, "Who moved it?" thinking that perhaps it was someone who did not know its purpose. Could it have been destroyed in Hurricane Matthew that had recently devastated so much of Haiti? But there it was down in a hollow "in case children should want a playhouse." It was clear. Needs, times, and solutions may change, but God's purpose is always to seek and save that which is lost—the orphans like Odes and Charles, the sick like Yolette, and the poor of spirit like Lulu. Wallace and I created Ti Kay to be a model for how the Haitians could build a house to survive a storm, but in the end God turned it into so much more: a place to meet Him and survive life's storms.

Not So In Haste, My Heart

Not so in haste, my heart!
Have faith in God and wait;
Although He linger long,
He never comes too late.

He never cometh late;
He knoweth what is best;
Vex not thyself in vain;
Until He cometh, rest.

Until He cometh, rest,
Nor grudge the hours that roll;
The feet that wait for God
Are soonest at the goal;

Are soonest at the goal
That is not gained by speed;
Then hold Thee still, my heart,
For I shall wait His lead.

Bradford Torrey

A FAMILY FOR ANTHONY

A Haitian boy named Anthony found a home as a result of two people who passed by the Mission on the Kenscoff Road. Martine was of French descent, in her mid-thirties, and teaching at the Union School in Port-au-Prince when we met. As so many would, Martine used the Mission as a retreat; whenever she needed a change, strengthening, or loving understanding, she came for a visit. We would sit in my living room by the fire, praying and crying together. Through listening and sharing with Martine over the next two years, Wallace and I became partners in her life.

I remember Martine praying for God to send more Christian teachers to the school and her hope for a husband and a family of her own. Imagine Wallace and my excitement when Martine announced that another Christian man was coming to teach at her school with a background in teaching on a Navajo reservation in the United States.

We tried not to get ahead of the Lord with matchmaking when we met Gary a few weeks later. He was forty-four years old and was teaching fourth grade at Union School. Gary told us that a motivating factor in deciding to come to Haiti was his desire to adopt since it was one of the last places where it was possible for a single man to do so. Thus, he was not in Haiti long before he visited an orphanage in central Haiti where all sixty children tried to teach him Creole. He loved them all, but especially an eight-year-old named Anthony.

Although it was a long, rough jeep ride to the orphanage over bad roads, Gary made several trips, taking Martine and other teachers from Union School to meet Anthony and give their input. As teachers, they were surprised that the orphanage was not also a school but more a place where children received food and a place to sleep. The teachers had stumbled onto the sad reality that orphanages in Haiti are too often a claim for soliciting money from foreign sponsors rather than a real home for the nurturing and teaching of children.

The teachers understood there would be some deep waters to cross if Gary decided to adopt Anthony who was undisciplined, illiterate, and only spoke Creole. The only affection he had ever known was from his grandmother who lived in a nearby community where he occasionally visited her for a night. As far as Anthony was concerned, everyone around him was someone to either play with or give him what he needed.

Gary's attitude was like the Haitian proverb, "Don't look for the bridge until you get to the river."

I don't know how much Gary and Martine talked about the adoption together, but Gary began the process, which would take months, and this gave him time to develop a relationship with Martine.

As soon as Gary was allowed, he brought Anthony to Port-au-Prince, and wise decisions were made for Anthony's educational, social, and emotional needs. Gary insisted that Anthony learn the English language, receive consistent discipline, and learn the importance of the authority figure. Martine helped Anthony with French, and both she and Gary taught him about the Christian faith.

Like so often, it seems to be God's way to lead us through twists, turns, ins, and outs, but little matters as long as we are sure we are being led. Martine had trusted God with the desires of her heart, so we were overjoyed when the happy couple announced their engagement and asked that Wallace perform the ceremony and that I organize the reception.

Gary and Martine were married in our backyard at the Mission on the Kenscoff Road in front of a small group of local friends. God had sent both Martine and Gary to the Mission, and through them provided a family for Anthony. Wallace and I were glad to be part of the blessing.

The Way

I had taken up a path
In early life, you see—
But all I found was wrath
Would shower down on me.

It wasn't 'till turned to God
His love and joy and good
'Twas in the soul—a gentle prod
Is when I understood.

God had never left me
He always was a part
Loving, yearning, waiting
In a corner of my heart.

Now we are together
I talk to Him each day
I pray in joy and wonder now
For me—He shows the way.

James Joseph Huesgen

TWO TREASURES

Wallace was an ordained minister, but he was also a treasure hunter. All through northern Haiti, where the French colonists had fled, there were wonderful stories of treasures buried at the time of the slave uprising. Stories were passed down from generation to generation about finding earthen-jars buried in gardens. Once, while reporting at the police station, I saw several sterling-silver plates, bowls, and a pitcher, stacked in the chief of police's office. When I asked, the chief explained that they were part of a treasure that had been found in a peasant's garden and no, they were not for sale. Later inquiry found that none of it had been returned to the peasant farmers, but no one knew the treasure's whereabouts. Rumors were that it could be seen in the home of the chief of police's mistress! After that, I believed the people who told us that any treasure found should be kept secret and never turned in to the police.

One of the most fascinating stories we heard was about a man named Sergeant Wirkus who, during the period of 1915-1934, was assigned to military duty on the little island of La Gonâve off the coast of Haiti. In his book *The White King of La Gonave* Wirkus explained how he learned the language and was accepted into the culture created from the union of Arawak Indian religions and African Vodou customs. Years later, friends of ours who remembered Wirkus confirmed that he was able to transport boat loads of sacred Arawak artifacts off the island because of his trusted position in their society. It was unlikely that any Arawak artifacts remained on La Gonâve after Wirkus left, but there was always the fascination that perhaps there were some remaining and we could find them, if we were willing to accept the challenge of searching for them.

Our missionary work gave us little opportunity to satisfy our curiosity. Then, a missionary couple serving at La Gonâve came to the Mission for a retreat. We became friends, and at the conclusion of their visit, they asked if we would come visit them someday. We enthusiastically said, "Yes!"

Our friends were delighted when we arranged to meet them with our sons. Knowing Wallace's enthusiasm, they had planned a treasure-hunting excursion. I kept insisting that I wished to find a carved stone amulet like our hostess wore. Wallace said, "Look for wood. If you find one piece of Arawak wood it is worth one hundred times more than a stone amulet." He knew that only three such pieces existed—two in the British museum and one in Trinidad.

The weather was hot the day we went exploring. The sun was relentless as were the mosquitoes, and the humidity was high, making the mid-day, four-hour-trek through the hills filled with cactus groves and coral boulders unbearable.

When we stopped to refresh ourselves in a village, we met an elderly native who was fascinated that white strangers could speak her language. She insisted we join her in the shade of the Acacia tree in her yard as she boiled an egg to share with Wallace. In the Haitian culture, eating together creates camaraderie, and soon she was answering my husband's questions about artifacts.

About seventy years ago, when she was a little girl, the elderly woman explained, she and her mother were passing through a part of the island called Twou Lanfè, Hell Hole. Her mother paused, needing to *ale akote*—go outside—behind a nearby bush growing in the midst of coral boulders.

Suddenly her mom screamed, "Run! Get out of here! The devil lives here! I can see his house!"

While squatting, her mother had stretched to look inside the mouth of a stone-formed shelter and had seen wooden furniture inside. She had thrown some pebbles inside and heard a bell-like *ting! ting!* She was sure it was the residence of the evilest spirit. She saw black pottery faces—we knew that meant it was a rare pottery brought from Puerto Rico by pre-Spanish Indian traders.

The story excited our interest, but we were out of time. Twou Lanfè was in a different area of the island, and we were scheduled to leave by boat early the next morning.

The next morning we were up at daybreak preparing to leave when our host came into our bedroom and said, "I've just received a message over the radio. High seas are expected due to a storm and your boat has been postponed until 2:00 p.m."

"Good!" Wallace exclaimed, seeing the delay as divine providence. "Let's go look for that treasure!"

Armed with two gunny sacks and a little cash to hire someone to guide us to Twou Lanfè we hurriedly set out. We found a constable who was not afraid of the evil spirits and set out for a two hour hike through rough, dry, cactus-filled countryside.

At Twou Lanfè, the cactus plants had become cactus vines determined to grab us and hold us back from getting over the coral boulders that must have been thrown up when erupting volcanoes made the island. It was easy to believe this was the home of evil spirits, as the land was so inhospitable. We searched and searched, but I didn't see a hole. Feeling like the task was impossible, I was about to give up when I heard my husband yell, "Here it is!"

Among the thorn bushes and cactus, we knelt down to look. There inside the hole we could see several items on flat coral slabs lodged in between boulders. Our guide reached into the hole and pulled out wooden trays, a stool, and a bowl. We were amazed as we looked at the items; because they were on rock slabs deep within the hole, the items had been spared from the effects of humidity and dry rot.

We didn't want to seem too excited as we might arouse suspicion with the constable who was our guide, so we complained in Creole that we had not found any pottery or other vessels we had hoped to find. He responded saying that he was immensely sorry that we hadn't found what we wanted and gave us police sanction to take the "old, undesirable wooden items." We all laughed together as he quoted the Haitian proverb, "To the hungry man, the intestine of the dried herring is meat." So it was that later that afternoon, when we took the boat back to the mainland, the items we found were part of our cargo.

When we got back to the Mission, we knew the first thing to do was determine the items' authenticity by taking photographs and sending them to the Museum of Natural History in New York City. While we were waiting for a reply, we kept the wooden items hidden amongst the linens in the big wood and forged-iron trunk in our house, continually wondering if it was wise, or safe, to do so as we heard stories of Tonton Macoutes raiding villages in search of unearthed treasure to sell. We were also careful not to show them to many people in case word got around to officials who would lay claim to them and they would disappear like so many of Haiti's historical treasures.

It was during this time that two men from Grande-Rivière-du-Nord came to the Mission with an interesting story and request. We knew that the church we had helped start was hoping to expand and needed additional funds to purchase a unique property that had come up for sale right on the town square. The fund for the land had been started two years before when an early convert's savings had been found after his death by his son.

While cleaning, his son had found a small suitcase made from old Mobil oil cans and tomato paste tins under his father's bed. When the son opened the suitcase he found dozens of pieces of paper with *"Pour Le Maitre," "*For the Master," written on them, and each paper held one to three gourds in Haitian currency. The modest sum was a beginning, but more was needed to purchase the desired property.

The two men who came to the Mission had a note from the Pastor that read, "You may trust these men that the story you are about to hear is real. It will endanger them if it becomes public. They bring to you a few echantiyon (samples)."

Imagine our surprise when we looked in a little bag that smelled of dust and sweat and saw sterling silver Spanish reales of every denomination that looked almost new. A church member had been plowing the land, preparing to plant, and had found jars filled with the coins. Fearful, he took them to his elderly pastor.

We knew that the story must be kept quiet. We would have to have the treasure evaluated and redeemed outside of Haiti. Wallace and I looked at each other and told the men we would help them.

Two weeks later the men returned, each carrying several pounds of reales. This time the coins were hidden in rough farmer's bags filled with mangoes. When stopped on the road, the men had said they were bringing the mangoes to the Mission as a gift.

We sorted the coins, paid the finder their value in present-day currency—a lot for him—and sold them to a man from an international NGO. The pastor was amazed at the amount of money they raised. The congregation was able to purchase land on the town square and praised God for His provision.

We at the Mission also rejoiced but wondered how in the world would the people ever be able to build a church equal to the prestigious location on the town square? In Luke 14:28-30 Jesus was teaching His disciples to count the cost and avoid ridicule of ever turning back from following him. Although building costs were greatly less in Haiti than in the United States, and the church people would do all the unskilled labor, many of the essential building materials would have to be imported and were costly. At that time, the per capita income of Haiti was $250 per year. If God wanted them to build that church, He would have to be the one to provide.

He did.

We had been waiting for a response from the Natural History Museum about the Arawak items we found, and finally one came. Our photos had been referred to Dr. Olsen, the Americas' specialist in Arawak culture. He contacted us, requesting permission to come inspect the items in person. When Dr. Olsen arrived, he was delighted to find the artifacts in better condition than he had anticipated and said the items should definitely become part of the exhibit at the Yale Museum. He offered to pay for the items. The amount was less than a private collector would have offered us, but we felt strongly that the items should go to an institutional museum rather than a private collection, which Dr. Olsen appreciated. We also told him about our desire to help the church at Grande-Rivière-du-Nord. And that is where God's final provision for the church came to be. What Dr. Olsen paid went to help build the church.

The church of Grande-Rivière-du-Nord is full of a new generation of believers bearing hope and light. They are soldiers looking forward, but also more and more interested in their history. Through the International Committee of Museums of United Nations of which the *Musée du Peuple* at the Mission is a member, there is a proposal that the Arawak artifacts may one day return to Haiti.

Handfuls of Purpose

"...but my trust is in the Lord, my God, and though in deep conflict and a vile sinner, I am not destroyed, and shall lose nothing in the furnace but dross. Jesus, my own Saviour, sits by, though not so visibly; His heart sympathizes, while mine is agonizing; and He will—oh, yes!—He will deliver."

Ruth Bryan

ENESIO

When Wallace and I met Enesio in Cuba, he wanted to return to Haiti to reconnect with his family. We met the young man because he wanted to practice speaking English, but it soon became clear that our acquaintance was divinely orchestrated. While talking, Enesio shared how his mother taught him about the Bible and the Living Word, Jesus Christ, and he lived out his faith, which was difficult under the atheistic government of Cuba. He expressed his desire to go to Haiti and find his great uncle.

Three days before Christmas, Enesio appeared at the Mission on the Kenscoff Road. He had a temporary visa and U.S. currency, both of which were hard to get. Knowing time was of the essence, Enesio was excited to find his great uncle as quickly as possible. The only problem was his only clues for the search were his family's name, an outdated picture of his uncle, and an address of "South Haiti." We knew we needed God's help, so we said a prayer and began searching.

The first miracle was when we found Enesio's cousin who told us that Great Uncle Willie was now Archbishop of South Haiti. Enesio would have to wait to meet his great uncle since he was currently in Rome. This presented a problem since Enesio's temporary visa expired before his great-uncle's return.

Enesio was determined to stay in Haiti, so when we got back to the Mission he immediately decided he would apply for a new visa. Enesio knew Cuba would not grant him another visa, so he thought he would apply for a United States visa at the American Consulate. He had to surrender his Cuban passport as part of the application process. If his application was approved, his passport would be returned to him along with the visa.

Enesio's passport was returned to him, but he had no visa, and what was worse was there was a stamp inside his Cuban passport that said APPLICATION REFUSED from the American Consulate. We knew that with that stamp inside Enesio's passport, he would be arrested immediately if he tried to enter Cuba.

Instead of being discouraged, Enesio decided to make himself useful. He learned Creole, improved his English, prayed, volunteered at the Mission, and learned more about Haiti. Enesio truly was a witness of God's grace in word and deed.

One day, a request for blood donors came from Dr. Bernard at the hospital. The Mission and its visitors were often called to give blood for emergency transfusions when there was an accident. In this case a little girl from the mountains was badly burned and her parents were too superstitious and too fearful to take her to the Red Cross blood center. Enesio wasted no time and immediately went to the hospital to give blood.

While there, Enesio met a Haitian woman who spoke Spanish. She was an affable Christian lady, and during their conversation she explained how she regularly went to the Dominican Republic to get salable commodities for her business in Haiti. She invited Enesio to her shanty to meet her friends and elderly mother. Enesio shared with them his desire to meet his great uncle and his current situation, so they had a time of prayer and sang songs of praise. The woman invited Enesio to go to the Dominican Republic with her the following morning by bus. She promised to help him find employment and legal papers. She asked for

Enesio's passport to secure a seat on the bus, and Enesio gave it to her. They agreed to meet each other at the bus station at 6:00 a.m.

Enesio didn't have a car or a license, so he asked a friend to drive him to the bus station. They were delayed by an overturned truck on the Kenscoff Road, so they arrived after the bus had left. They tried to overtake the bus unsuccessfully; when they arrived at the border, the bus had already passed. There was another bus Enesio could get on, but he had no passport and his name was not on the bus driver's list of passengers. However, Enesio did have his United State's currency with him. In a country where border bribes are common, you can guess what came next. The negotiations took almost all of Enesio's U.S. currency, but he got on the bus as one of the thirty-eight Haitians on the driver's list. At this point, Enesio's only identification was a Cuban driver's license and a copy of his University of Havana's Engineering diploma.

The usual procedure of the Dominican police at each inspection point was to greet the load of passengers, look around, write down the name of the bus and plaque number, and wish them all a safe trip. This happened at the first three inspection points. At the fourth inspection point after the usual procedure, a second policeman came onto the bus yelling, "I want to check every person's identification!" Poor Enesio. The police arrested him and sent him back over the border to Haiti where he was imprisoned at the border station, Mal Pas, and a detailed police report was sent to Port-au-Prince, to the head immigration office.

We knew nothing of the incident until Saturday when the police allowed Enesio to call the Mission saying he was at Mal Pass. Wallace and I wanted to have Enesio released to our charge, but the only man with the authority to grant our request was the chief of immigration in Port-au-Prince and he probably wasn't in his office since it was Saturday. We prayed and decided to make the call anyway.

God miraculously had the chief answer the phone! We asked him if we could drive to Mal Pass and have Enesio released to our charge. We were thankful for the Mission's reputation of integrity when the chief granted our request, saying he would send a note to Mal Pass, and that we were to have Enesio in his office at 9:00 Monday morning.

Early Sunday we drove the two hours to Mal Pass where we were well-received by the officer on duty who verified the chief of immigration had given instruction to release Enesio to our custody. The officer also allowed us to read the official report that had been forwarded to the main office. We were shocked at the severity of the charges listed and recognized not only the seriousness of Enesio's situation, but also the miracle taking place in his release. The guards brought Enesio to us—frightened, hungry, and ashamed, but happy to see us, and glad to be out of prison.

As we drove back to the Mission, Enesio could tell us only bits and pieces about the woman who now had his passport. He asked if we could take him to her mother's shanty. The shanty was located in one of Haiti's many slums, where cardboard, plywood, and tin made up the living quarters and muddy, pot-holed walking paths were the streets that created a labyrinth in which it was easy to get lost. We agreed to take Enesio to the slum, but knew there was little hope of success.

The road eventually became too narrow for the car, so Wallace stayed with the car while Enesio and I got out to walk. We walked past the shanties. There were no road names, so we just tried to keep our bearings as Enesio tried to remember where he had gone a few days before.

Suddenly an elderly woman sleeping outside her shanty jumped up, raised both her hands heavenward, and began praising God. She exclaimed, "I knew you were coming! I've been praying for you all night. God told me you would come! Praise God!"

She gestured for us to follow her to the doorway of her shanty where she disappeared inside. We heard the rustling of papers and thuds of items shifting, then she appeared again—carrying Enesio's passport. What a miracle!

Without knowing Haiti, without having experienced the broken promises of friends, or knowing the value of foreign passports, the difficulties caused by lack of telephones and other communication, and the prevalence of banditry and greed, you might miss some of the wonder and greatness of what God did. I never did understand how the passport made it back to the old mother. The basic gist was that when the lady arrived at the border she bribed the driver of a small motorcycle taxi to take the passport back to her mother who lived in an overcrowded area with no address—no location, no street, no number—nothing. There is no way such a thing could have happened without God's miraculous intervention.

We returned to the Mission and prepared for the meeting with the chief of immigration in Port-au-Prince the following morning. Our appointment was at 9:00 a.m. We arrived early and were shown to the chief's office where we waited...and waited. Finally, the chief arrived. He greeted us and asked his assisting officers and even his secretary to leave the office.

When the three of us were alone, he sat down at his desk, opened the file, and reviewed with us the illegality of the case. He said he was kindly disposed toward the Mission but could not help us. International law clearly states that a foreigner who commits a crime in a foreign country must be returned to his own country immediately.

Both Enesio and I knew that he would be imprisoned once he returned to Cuba because of his expired visa and passport with the red stamp of the United State's refused request. Enesio and I both bowed our heads at the same moment and began to pray to God.

While Enesio's head was still bowed, I began to implore the Director, "Sir, I understand your position completely. Let me assure you, however, that Enesio is not a criminal. He is a good person who was giving blood to a needy child when he met a new friend who took his passport. He is new in Haiti, but his family was originally from Haiti and he is here looking for his family roots. The reason Enesio is still in Haiti is because he is waiting for his great-uncle Monseigneur Romeleus, Archbishop of Jeremie, to return from Rome."

At this the Director learned forward on his desk and looked intently into my eyes. "Madame Wallace, if what you say is true, this man, Enesio, is my wife's relative. Monseigneur Romeleus is already back in Haiti and wishes to speak with him. My wife, then, would be Enesio's cousin. She works as Monseigneur Romeleus' secretary. Excuse me." Then the director quietly dialed his phone, spoke softly, and handed the phone to Enesio saying, "Here, speak with your cousin."

As Enesio talked to his cousin and then his great uncle, the director gently closed the file on Enesio and put it in the desk drawer.

Eventually Enesio became a legal resident in Haiti and worked at the Mission on the Kenscoff Road. His Spanish speaking skills proved very useful when the Mission reached out to share the Good News with Spanish-speaking visitors. He helped us identify those who were professing Christians, those who were not opposed, and others who enjoyed the Mission and the kindness of the people who lived there but were atheists. For as Jesus said, "You did not choose Me, but I chose you and appointed you that you should go and bear fruit, and that your fruit should remain, that whatever you ask the Father in My name He may give you" John 15:16. In everything Enesio did, he was a positive witness of God's love and grace.

But grow in the grace and knowledge of our Lord and Savior Jesus Christ. To him be the glory both now and to the day of eternity. Amen.

2 Peter 3:18

YOU BETCHA

Steve was scarcely eighteen-years-old when the director of the Union Gospel Mission Camp in Minnesota sent him to experience life on the Kenscoff Road in Haiti. Working with hundreds of needy youth in the Twin Cities of Minnesota, the Union Gospel Mission Camp sought to guide men of the Christian faith with meaningful productivity and purpose. During several summers, young Steve benefited from the camp, learned to be helpful, and eventually was given an opportunity to serve on an internship training trip at the Mission.

It was time for the beardless, rosy-cheeked, soft-skinned boy to become a man and be responsible. Without much warning or preparation, Steve arrived in this new overseas world and met his mentor, my husband, Wallace. Steve noticed immediately that Wallace always seemed to be overworked with no time to waste, and Wallace hoped the young man would be a competent, trustworthy helper.

Steve went from the flatlands of Minnesota to the 5,000 foot high mountains, from Minnesota's ice and snow to Haiti's tropical heat, from orderly, stern Scandinavians to friendly, unhurried Haitians. Everyone always seemed able to talk, but none appeared to listen. Steve received a paper booklet marked "Dictionary" and a wide-brim palm leaf straw hat. Then his internship began—he had a lot to digest.

The morning after Steve arrived, Wallace had an urgent need for a truck driver to get provisions for seventy men who were attending a training session at the Leaders Institute at the Mission. One of the provisions needed was beef. The only beef market was miles away in La Croix des Bouquets where local entrepreneurs filled the role of cowboy. Some of these cowboys traveled long distances with herds of four to eight cows, horns tied together by long hand-twisted sisal ropes. Bargaining was done on site, as was the slaughtering of the animals, so that the market crowd could buy fresh meat whacked off with a machete.

Poor Steve knew nothing of it, of Haiti's cowboys or meat markets. So he was a little surprised when Wallace asked him, "Can you drive a truck?" Steve looked at the truck—an old Chevrolet body placed on a metal frame with decent tires. He squared his shoulders and replied, "You betcha." It was the first of many times Wallace would hear that confident, decisive answer to his request for help.

Wallace handed Steve the keys with the following instruction and warning. "Jannot will be your guide. He knows where to go and he will negotiate the price of the beef. Be careful. Keep your hand on the money deep inside your pocket. Watch carefully; look out for pick pockets. Do you think you'll be all right?" Steve started the motor and replied, "Yep, you betcha!" and drove away.

Jannot guided Steve, bought the cow, and arranged its slaughter. Steve helped him load several large laundry tubs filled with pieces of the cow wrapped in big sheets of plastic into the truck.

Upon Steve's return, one of his first exclamations was, "They killed it right there! Man, I tell you we got it all. We got everything—I mean everything—even the hide and the tail, and also the intestines. The other parts he exclaimed over included the four legs from the hooves to the knee and the big black and white head, including the curved horns. At the market place, the legs were usually placed into big cauldrons and boiled long enough for the skin and tendons to become jellylike. The bare bones were then bought by artisans to dry, scrape, and polish into imitation ivory for decorative facing and jewelry. The horns were also bought by artisans to make polished onyx-like decorative facings on jewelry boxes.

Steve lived with us like a member of the family. He would often join me in the kitchen for a cup of coffee and ask, "Mom, how is the old goat this morning? What is he butting today?" "Old Goat" was the nickname Steve gave to Wallace. Steve noticed it was difficult to get more than a few words from Wallace because his mentor was always dealing with the day's urgent plans, directives, and unforeseen events. Still, Steve observed the tenacity with which Wallace "butted" against things that were not true, honorable, right, pure, lovely, and good, as quoted in Philippians 4:8 and the nickname "Old Goat" was born. Life with Steve became so easy; he was just like one of the family. He quickly picked up the Creole language and was as free with the locals as he was with Wallace and me.

Steve was there when the cook suggested that a real treat would be soup *tet kabrit*—goat head soup. It's considered a special dish for the Haitians and is served in well-appreciated restaurants. The cook was startled when I questioned her choice and responded that it was written in the recipe book. Recipe, or not, I wasn't sure that our guests' pallets would appreciate the cook's choice. When she made the soup, most of us did not call it delicious. However, the bleached goat's skull that was the soup's centerpiece made a great joke later when we concealed it under a cake cover as a good-bye gift for a volunteer.

Steve not only found himself in Haiti, he also found his wife Cindy as well. Cindy was a short-term missionary on the island of

La Gonave in the bay of Haiti. We requested that Steve take Cindy for an early morning Jeep ride to a neighboring community before she went to the airport. While rendering the short service, he bemoaned the idea that she was on her way out. As Cindy rushed off to the airport, Steve sneaked into our office and copied Cindy's full name and address from the Mission's Guest Book. Only they could tell us about finding yourself and finding one another through finding God.

Years later, we laughed with them, sharing memories at their home in the US with their two bright, ambitious sons, their three beautiful daughters, and one loudly yelping dog. We talked about life as Steve had known it in Haiti, the people, and the call of God. Then we joined in the cook-out with Steve's next-door neighbors as they made plans for launching a program for needy people in Haiti. Later, we exchanged gifts.

I had bought my gifts at the Iron Market in Haiti. The now-famous wrought iron structure for the market was initially intended to go to Egypt to become the railway station. When the sale fell through, the structure was purchased by President Florvil Hyppolite in 1891 to help modernize Port-au-Prince. The Iron Market's *machann yo*, or vendors, sold everything from *frescos*, or snow cones, to beautiful carvings, many made of animal bones, like those of the cow Steve drove back to the Mission all those many years ago. Not everyone enjoys searching for unusual and rare woodcarvings, but I do, particularly in the Iron Market. One of my most rewarding finds was what I presented to Steve and Wallace that day: two pairs of bookends made of light and dark wood beautifully carved into goat heads. One pair was a gift to Steve, the "Yes! You betcha I can!" who had been sent to Haiti to "find himself" and the other to Wallace, Steve's 92-year-old mentor who still butts his head against whatever is contrary to Philippians 4:8.

I lift up my eyes to the hills.
From where does my help come?
My help comes from the Lord,
Who made heaven and earth.

Psalm 121:1-2

CHICKEN GEORGE

We truly believe people were sent to the Mission on the Kenscoff Road by God to fulfill a specific purpose. In some we immediately saw the answer to our prayers, and in others, God's purpose was slowly revealed. Regardless, we are so thankful for the obedience people showed in coming to the Mission, using their gifts for God's glory. So many individuals like this come to mind. One is George, who we affectionately named "Chicken George."

George came to us at a time when Canada was sending whole grain wheat to be milled in Haiti so that a loaf of bread would be affordable for all the people. Another positive outcome of this new endeavor, in addition to there being more food for the people, was the byproduct of the milling process, called wheat shorts. These were now available at prices low enough for peasant farmers to use them for animal feed. At that time, poultry husbandry skills were not prevalent among the Haitian people, so we prayed for God to send someone to help us educate our neighbors about raising chickens.

He did.

George was retired from the DeKalb Corn Company and had spent his entire career as an expert in various departments of the company's poultry section. A quiet, very humble Christian man, George had prayed that God would use him in retirement to help needy people.

Before Chicken George came, any chickens the people had ran loose, were rarely fed or watered, and thus were malnourished. Chicken George reached out to the people and through various demonstrations taught them how to make and use chicken pens, carry water from distant sources, and give it to the chickens, as well as how to use wheat shorts to make nutritious feed, gather and count eggs, and evaluate the age and worth of each chicken.

He imported specially chosen, one-day-old chicks from a Mennonite friend and watched over them in the Mission brooder house. Those who took the class were each given twenty chickens when the chickens were old enough to lay eggs. There was a limitless market for the fine, large, fresh brown eggs. Then when hens were old, they were sold for meat and the farmer was expected to pay the price for twenty new fresh layers.

It was a good project—families bought shoes and put their children in school and young couples even got married because with "egg money" a young man could build a small, simple, two-room house. Chicken George built a rapport with every person who took his class. He often walked hours over steep mountain trails to verify a project, diagnose a potentially threatening poultry epidemic, and administer technical help of all kinds. Through the years, it became more and more difficult for this tall, emaciated-looking man with shaky knees and shortness of breath to keep up with the demands. It was fortunate that he had two young local "disciples" to carry on after cancer eventually took him home to heaven.

Often, because George could not speak Creole, he could not tell the people how much he loved them and how proud he was of their success, but with his enormous false-tooth smile he said much more than that.

Learning of his death, a Haitian pastor said, "When the Book of Life is opened, the angel will find the name CHICKEN GEORGE written in bold letters."

One Day at a Time!

One day at a time, with its failures and fears,
With its hurts and mistakes, with its weakness and tears,
With its portion of pain, and its burden of care;
One day at a time, we must meet and must bear.

One day at a time, to be patient and strong,
To be calm under trial, and sweet under wrong;
Then its toiling shall pass, and its sorrow shall cease;
It shall darken and die, and the night shall bring peace.

One day at a time—but the day is so long,
And the heart is not brave, and the soul is not strong,
O piteous Christ, be near all the way;
Give courage and patience, and strength for the day.

Swift comes His answer, so clear and so sweet;
"Yes, I'll be with you, your troubles to meet;
I will not forget you, nor fail you, nor grieve;
I will not forsake you; I never will leave."

Not yesterday's load, we are called on to bear,
Nor the morrow's uncertain and shadowy care;
Why should we look forward, or back with dismay?
Our needs, as our mercies, are but for the day.

One day at a time, and the day is His day;
He has numbered its hours, though they haste or delay.
His grace is sufficient, we walk not alone;
As the day, so the strength that He gives His own.

Annie Johnson Flint

TOM'S PIGS

Ww were in the middle of a crisis concerning pigs when Tom and Pat came to the Mission—he to help with agriculture and she to teach in our Self Help project. Nearly every rural family, no matter how poor, had a pig, and not for the reason you might think. In Haiti, as gross as it may seem, the pig was the family's toilet. At the clinic, a mother often explained how sick her child was by stating how many times he had squatted in front of the pig that day. The Haitian people considered the pigs' clean-up efforts the least messy, dirty, and smelly means of disposal. The pig also represented the family's bank account as it could be sold for burials, weddings, and to pay the houngan for Vodou services to appease the ancestral spirits.

The razor-backed breed of pigs had survived from colonial days. The breed was resistant to parasites and resilient in spite of inadequate food and water. Then the swine fever virus was found moving downriver from the Dominican Republic. The United States Department of Agriculture and the Canadian government believed that only drastic measures would prevent the swine fever from entering North and South America. Their proposed plan was to destroy all pigs in Haiti—every single one. Eventually the

Haitian government agreed to the plan provided that each family be well paid for any pig found on their property.

Immediately, protests erupted. Leftist organizations stated that the "capitalist nations were determined in their plans to oppress and destroy the underdeveloped countries of Latin America," increasing anti-American sentiments. Haitians were told that the new-promised pigs would never do well, and this situation was all a way for North America to make more money at the Haitian people's expense.

The Mission on the Kenscoff Road became an important component in the successful reintroduction of the pigs. We were determined to show the Haitian people that the new pigs would integrate well. Working together, our son Wally and Tom worked out an amazing program of great detail. Multiple pig breeding stations were established in each community to care for the pigs, and classes on how to care for, keep, feed, and breed the new pigs were made available to the peasants in every part of Haiti.

We knew that Tom had not come to the Mission but had been sent. His expertise and constant oversight made the project a success. The sows were birthing twelve to sixteen piglets to the point where pigs seemed to be outracing Haiti's rampant population growth. The piglets had to remain with their mother until they reached a certain age, then they were issued by age and sex to Haitians who had passed the animal husbandry class—making sure there was a male for every certain number of female pigs in each community.

From early morning until late at night, both men and women were waiting in line to collect the pigs. Have you ever heard a caught pig yell? We couldn't miss it! The blood-curdling squealing of the young, captured pigs, the deep hooking threats of the mother pigs, and the loud talking, debating, and happy laughter of the mountain people made for noisy days at the Mission. Some young pigs were put into gunny sacks to be carried over steep foot trails to their new home. Others were held down while each pair of front and back legs were tied together—first the two front legs, then the two back legs, and the new owner would have someone help him balance the pig's body around the back of his neck. With one pair of legs tightly held in each hand, the rebellious pig eventually quieted-down and looked almost happy riding on the back side of his new master's neck.

Usually the pigs put in gunny sacks found a way to repeatedly leap upward in the sack while making pathetic squeals of desperation. This picture inspired a local pastor's sermon, where he talked about fleeing from temptation: "A man should not walk behind a girl in a tight skirt causing her backside to rotate up and down like two pigs in a sack!"

Over the next two years more than 2,000 families in the area got a new start with foreign pigs. Actually, the foreign pigs adapted well to the weeds, eventually adjusted to being staked on the end of a rope, and many learned to wait for the morning visit of each family member. Some farmers even complained that the new pigs "had too many babies" as they could not afford the feed or water for them. Now cooked pig meat is piled high on roadside stands where it is peddled to passers-by. It is no longer just at weddings and funerals that the people get a small bit of *griot*, deep-fried cubes of pork, drenched in *piklis*, Haiti's wonderful, extremely hot cabbage relish, and one of the greatest treats in the world.

Giving

God gives us joy that we may give;
He gives us joy, that may share;
Sometimes he gives us loads to lift,
That we may learn to bear.
For life is gladder when we give,
And love is sweeter when we share,
And heavy loads rest lightly too,
When we have learned to bear.

Author Unknown

GINNY'S DUNGEON

For Virginia (Ginny) every year started with her loading a van full of supplies in St. Paul, Minnesota, and driving it to Florida. She had once been a missionary in Nigeria, but due to family responsibilities had returned to the U.S. where she lived and worked as a nurse anesthetist. Now in her retirement, she annually volunteered at the Mission. Each year, Ginny started loading the van in St. Paul from floor to ceiling with supplies. She would get the supplies from Good Will, dollar stores, hospitals, and friends. She brought medical supplies as well as clothing for the twenty-two children she and her friends were sponsoring in Haiti to go to school.

In loading the van, Ginny would leave a few inches of ceiling space, enough for her to crawl and lie down in, and that is where this dear woman would sleep on the several day trip to Florida. At night while en route to Florida she would stop at the highway rest stop to use their facilities and sleep in the van on top of the load. She did all the driving, and to save cargo space she took no companion with her. She had special arrangements to leave the van three to four months in Florida with the Missionary Flights International people who are among those continuing to marvel at the amount of supplies Ginny took with her.

I remember the year Ginny sought out Christmas decorations from nursing homes and churches to bring to the Mission. She salvaged used artificial Christmas trees, garlands, lights, and other Christmas decorations, and when she got to the Mission, she put a lighted Christmas tree in the nurses' station. It caused a sensation among the patients and visitors but also jealousy among the other departments who complained that they had no Christmas trees. Ginny knew what she had to do. When she went back to St. Paul, she collected more Christmas decorations until the TB Center, Out-Patient Clinic, Pharmacy, and all the other departments had their own small or medium tree with lights. Many of the Nativity sets displayed in the *Musée du Peuple* at the Mission were brought by Ginny. She also was a genius at making something from anything and brought craft supplies with her. She taught several people in the mountain community how to make saleable crafts. But the greatest part of what Ginny did was never seen.

Ginny brought supplies to the Mission, but she wasn't the only one, and many of the medical supply donations ended up in a place we nicknamed "The Dungeon" to be sorted "later." No one wanted to tackle sorting through all of those boxes. Until Ginny volunteered to tackle "The Dungeon." The tons of medical equipment and supplies were taken from "The Dungeon" and moved to a spacious consolidated storehouse. There, Ginny opened cases, accessed, sorted, and often with difficulty, identified tons of donated medical items. This storehouse became Ginny's territory and she guarded it as fiercely as any lion. There was no doubt she knew what to do, how to do it, and when to do it.

The only problem was that Ginny took invasion of her territory personally. She heard the best when wearing both her hearing aids and didn't talk much. She was not sure what had been said so was wisely quiet, but it gave her plenty of time to think, imagine, and wonder what people were saying, and why. This allowed misunderstandings, incorrect interpretations, and hurt feelings. Sometimes there was resentment, accusations, and threats to quit. I remember the time she arrived in Haiti with two American farmhouse-type brooms and mops as she felt the Haitian pioneer-bundle style broom "didn't really get it clean." My nearest battle with Ginny came when I used her broom to sweep a hospital ward and "took all those nasty germs back to her storeroom." Despite these moments of friction, I agreed with Dr. Bernard who said, "There was no instrument to measure the knowledge she had in her head or the love of God she had in her heart."

It was only at the age of eighty, that Ginny finally submitted to the urging of her family and friends and agreed to make her last trip to the Mission on the Kenscoff Road. When I see her brooms and mops, as well as the unopened crates in the hospital store room, I still think of her .

The righteous will flourish like palm trees
they will grow like a cedar in Lebanon.

Planted in the Lord's Temple,
they will flourish in the courtyard of our God.

They will still bear fruit even in old age;
they will be luxuriant and green.

They will proclaim: "The Lord is upright;
my rock, in whom there is no injustice."

Psalm 92:12-15

DETERMINED TO SERVE

L eah was eighty-two the first time she came to the Mission on the Kenscoff Road. We met her son Dan while he was filming a documentary for us. He mentioned he'd like to see his mom come help out at the Mission. We thought that was a reasonable idea since she was currently a missionary in Asia affiliated with Youth for Christ. However, when we learned she was eighty-two, we doubted she would find a place among the hard-working missionary staff or that she would be happy in the isolated environment with little social life. We questioned if it would be wise for her to be so far away from her family and friends. Would she be healthy in a land with no Medicare, plenty of diseases, and restricted food menus? We felt we did not have time to spare from our busy missionary lives to create activities for "an old volunteer lady."

Well, we were wrong on all counts. Leah turned out to be a prim, well-dressed, culturally elite widow who was determined to continue serving the Lord. Leah willingly and patiently completed hours of sorting anything and everything: sixty pounds of odd buttons that had been sent to the Mission and huge boxes of Christmas cards with foreign addresses that needed to be removed. Cards with illustrations of the Christmas story were put aside to use as gifts to share the true meaning of Christmas with those who had never heard the Good News, nor received a Christmas card. The cards with only words, as well as the blank second page on all of them, were packaged separately to use for Vacation Bible School hands-on projects.

Leah often spoke of her "consecrated needle." Churches in the United States sent us countless and constant barrels of used clothing, and many of the garments required simple alterations. Leah never complained about the hours she spent ripping and re-sewing. From one wonderful "Mother Hubbard-style" pantaloon she found beautiful hand-embroidered eyelet lace from which she made a wedding veil for Elvera who lived close to the Mission. She wasted nothing and was delighted to learn from the Haitian women, who often did not have sewing thread, that one could make thread for needle work by fraying out the last thread along the torn or cut edge of the cloth.

One could always find Leah in the one part of the Mission house she kept meticulously clean and orderly and claimed as her department. Noises of the Mission—meetings, visitors, etc., didn't bother her as she refused to use her hearing aid and electively kept her non-hearing ear in the direction of the hall.

Despite our initial concern, Leah stayed healthy and was adamant that the rest of us follow her lead and eat the strings from inside the banana pealing, nurture the dandelions for they were "good food," and use her liver medicine made from papaya seeds. Sometimes we wondered if she was teaching the herb doctors of Haiti or if they were teaching her. There was, however, a great difference as the local *medsen fèy* (leaf doctors) often mixed superstition and sorcery in with their treatments. Not Leah! Leah told everyone that her real doctor was Doctor Jesus.

Leah was never idle, never interrupted, never sought attention, and never needed help until 7:00 p.m. each evening when the staff dinner was finished. It was then that dear Leah would shuffle to one or several of the missionaries asking, "Will someone play with me?" She loved table games, could usually beat any of the group, and always encouraged us with her humor and spiritual tidbits. Sometimes everyone seemed to have other plans and Leah had no recourse but to go to Wallace with a heartbreaking whine, "Nobody wants to play with me tonight!"

It was not until she reached ninety that Leah no longer came to Haiti. We missed the labor of her hands, her delightful humor, wise instructions, and the twinkle of her eyes, and still to this day, whenever one is lonely or bored, we imitate Leah's whine, "Nobody wants to play with me..."

Even the youths shall faint and be weary, and the young men shall utterly fall: But they that wait upon the Lord shall renew their strength; they shall mount up with wings as eagles; they shall run, and not be weary; and they shall walk, and not faint.

–Isaiah 40:30-31

I RECKON' SO

When Clyde came as one of those who passed by, he brought his well-worn khaki and denim work clothes, his much-used farmer's hat, and thank God he brought his high-top plow shoes. He thought he would be helping clean out springs and dig wells in efforts to get much needed water to the people. He knew diarrhea caused by unclean water killed one in ten children under the age of five in Haiti, and he wanted to help.

Like so often happened, it soon became clear that Clyde was another of those who had not come but had been sent. A mission station needed to be established near the big lake, Letang Saumatre, but the acquired land was a thicket of every kind of cactus—tall, short, and creeping, as well as the wonderfully stately candelabra tree, but all of it was full of awful thorns. Mixed with the cactus was years of brush and weeds, which gave harbor to hordes of stinging wasps.

There was no way that machetes and axes could clear the land, but a bulldozer might be rented if someone could drive it ten miles to the site and set about clearing. I remember asking Clyde if he could drive a bulldozer. His look of determination humbled me, and without further question he said, "I reckon so...." The local people had never seen anything like it—for weeks Clyde bulldozed through solid cactus thickets and dug out roots of the wonderful, old acacia trees which had been burned into charcoal. He raised great clouds of dust that settled on his sweat-wet clothing and layered over him. That dirty old hat only partially protected his bushy graying hair and only because he had those heavy, thick boots could he get to the heaps of cacti he piled up to set on fire. Working with the old tractor was not easy, and he would spend hours in 100+ degree heat, keeping it repaired and working, all the while managing the pain in his leg that was still healing from being smashed in a motorboat accident.

When asked, "How was the day?" the nearest to a complaint was, "Them damned wasps 'bout made me sick..." Removing his sweaty, old hat, we could see his eyes swollen from wasp stings. After washing off discoloring layers of dust, one often saw that his face and arms were swollen and almost raw.

Anyone could soon guess that Clyde had not always led a strict, disciplined life, but when questioned, he preferred to tell you about his church in California, and his faith and commitment to Jesus Christ who had not only forgiven his past, but put purpose and meaning into his life. Clyde did not speak often, and much of what he said was prefaced by, "As my Pa told me..." then he would say something like, "Nobody ain't never learned anything with his mouth open." He never learned Creole, but the Haitian people felt they understood him and responded to his brusque manner urging them to "get to work" and to "treat the lady-folks better" and his bellow of disgust and anger when anyone showed signs of shelfishness or shirking their duties.

If anyone ever thought that a missionary was a spineless, goodie-goodie, nerdy freak, they never met Clyde who left his mark both in the land he bulldozed and in the hearts of the Haitian people he loved.

Midst those with greed of gain,
They would not harken to My voice,
But scoffed with one accord;
Our labor never is in vain
If done unto the Lord.
Have courage, then, My faithful one,
I suffered all the way,
Thy sensitive and loving heart
I understand today;
Whate'er thy grief, what're thy care,
Just bring it unto Me.
Yea, in thy day of trouble, call,
I will deliver thee.

Susanne C. Umlaug

GOD'S TIME, RIGHT TIME

With white skin and blond hair, Dorit was easy to see in a church packed with 600 Haitians. I knew that she was not just a curious tourist because she joined in the joyous, passionate singing of the hymns in both Creole and French. After the service, I pushed my way through the crowd leaving the church to meet the pretty, young stranger. It turned out that Dorit was visiting a young Haitian student and had found the Mission on the Kenscoff Road. When she asked me, "Is there anything I can do to help?" I knew that she was the object lesson of the little song, God's time—right time—always on time... and that every child of God fills a special place in his plan. We knew that Dorit had been sent to the Mission as an answer to our prayer to help write up some of the Mission's important, overdue documents for the government of Haiti. Realizing the importance of just the right presentation and being unable to complete the documents in French with the balance of audacious demands and flowery humility needed, we had prayed for help. Then Dorit appeared in the hills of Haiti having freshly completed her PhD in International Communications in German, French, and English.

After working with us in Haiti, Dorit was convinced that God had a special project for her, and she worked closely with the African Christian community in Germany. She became a voice for Haiti, and especially the Mission on the Kenscoff Road. There is no way that the ministry and needs of the Mission on the Kenscoff Road could ever have been known in Germany if Dorit had not been among those who passed by.

Drinking From My Saucer

I don't have a lot of riches,
and sometimes the going's tough.
But I've got loved ones around me,
and that makes me rich enough.

I thank God for his blessings,
and the mercies He's bestowed.
I'm drinking from my saucer,
'cause my cup has overflowed.

I remember times when things went wrong,
my faith wore somewhat thin.
But all at once the dark clouds broke,
and the sun peeped through again.

So God, help me not to gripe about
the tough rows that I've hoed.
I'm drinking from my saucer,
'cause my cup has overflowed.

If God gives me strength and courage,
when the way grows steep and rough.
I'll not ask for other blessings,
I'm already blessed enough.

And may I never be too busy,
to help others bear their loads.
Then I'll keep drinking from my saucer,
'Cause my cup has overflowed.

John Paul Moore

COFFEE AND
THE FIRST LADY

A lthough Madame Dumarsais Estimé was First Lady of Haiti when I arrived, and the Mission on the Kenscoff Road was still being established, neither President Estimé or his beautiful, cultured wife had ever visited. In those early years it was not part of the "high society" to know or to mix with rural areas. The only part of that society to know Kenscoff were a few "old families" who traditionally sought respite from the heat of Port-au-Prince a few weeks each summer in the cool of the mountains. Then there was a military coup d'état in the 1950s and the Estimes escaped to New York City. It wasn't until Madame Estimé became Haiti's Ambassador to France that a mutual friend brought her to her first and only visit to the Mission on the Kenscoff Road. Maybe she never returned because of the coffee I served.

The terrible incident began when Melizan took the afternoon off to go to a wedding and I had no household help. In keeping with a deep-rooted Haitian tradition to serve coffee, I brought out the china demitasse coffee set that was reserved for the most special occasions. Once Madame and my friend were comfortable, I excused myself, anxious to "do the right thing." I felt saved when I saw some coffee left in a pan near the stove. Whee! I arranged the sweet biscuits on the pretty silver tray and was glad it didn't take long for the coffee to heat as I was embarrassed to be absent from my special visitors.

In proper manner, I poured the coffee into the china cup for each person, then waited as each person added her own sugar, and began to sip her coffee. Before sipping my own cup of coffee, I served the biscuits and chatted about the incomparable Haitian coffee, which I was sure Madame Estimé was missing while living in France. I did begin to wonder at her hesitant agreement with me and her mentioning that, "the poor people sometimes dry their coffee on the ground which gives it a musty taste."

Eventually, I tasted my own cup of coffee and suddenly realized what we were drinking was not coffee at all. I was shocked into silence. We were drinking black water made by soaking the dried local mushrooms! Before leaving for the wedding, Melizan had soaked the mushrooms in preparation for making black rice, a favorite, for dinner that evening.

With this realization, what could I do? Confess that I had just given black mushroom water to the ex-First Lady of Haiti, the current ambassador to France? Worry if there was anything about pure black mushrooms that would make them sick or cause internal fungus? Actually, I suggested we have a word of prayer for wisdom and blessing for the Ambassador before they left. During the prayer, I was silently asking God to not let the ladies be sick or keel over after visiting the Mission on the Kenscoff Road!

Life isn't about waiting for the storm to pass...
It's about learning to dance in the rain.

Author Unkown

SENT VIA MOTORCYCLE

While most visitors were glad for their time at the Mission, sometimes people were sent contrary to their wishes, and certainly contrary to their plans. It was almost supper time when our son, David, came in. While washing up, he explained that he was late because he had been helping a stranger whose motorcycle was broken down on the road. "Is it possible for an American stranger to have supper and stay overnight with us?" he asked. Of course the stranger could stay for supper! Of course we would fix a bed where he could stay until the old rented motorcycle could be repaired.

The young American man, Michael, explained that he had arrived as a tourist, had rented a motorcycle, and was exploring fifteen miles up the mountain. In the late afternoon, the old motorcycle broke down across from the Mission on the Kenscoff Road. Night was coming, making Michael apprehensive to be a foreign white man alone with no ability to communicate or get the motorcycle running. Some local people sent for David who was a certified mechanic. David went out to meet Michael, who was relieved when he heard David ask in English, "What's the trouble? Can I help you?" Neither David nor Michael could get the motorcycle started, so they pushed the cycle into the shop, hoping that they could fix it the next day.

During supper, Mike explained that he had no job and was recuperating from a terrible accident while at West Point. He hardly knew why he was in Haiti. In Miami, he was informed that he had missed the plane to Jamaica, but there was a flight to Haiti if he wanted to take it. He knew no one, knew nothing to do, and nothing about the country. When he arrived, he was surprised to discover that the people were not English speaking and he had been unable to get a map of the roads or towns. Michael kept saying how glad he was that David had appeared as Michael had heard about Vodou—about zombies, and evil spirits. We answered his questions about Haiti and why we were there, and Wallace gave him a short course in local beliefs and traditions. When Mike asked, "Well, what about all the people who do not accept Jesus Christ?" Wallace answered succinctly, "They are zombies. They are the walking dead!"

Shortly after supper Mike asked Wallace, "Would you please take a walk with me? There is so much I need to know." Together they found a quiet place on the Mission campus near the church where they could sit down. Mike said, "Sir, I want you to know that I am one of those living dead you spoke about. What can I do?" Having been close to physical death, Mike could understand spiritual death. That night Mike prayed in repentance, yielded himself to God, and experienced Jeremiah 29:13: "You will seek me and find me when you search for me with all your heart."

The next day Mike and David could not fix the motorcycle, so they returned it to Port-au-Prince. Mike stayed two weeks at the Mission on the Kenscoff Road. We all knew that Mike had not "come"—he had been sent, and he had also been halted. Mike returned to the United States to follow up with the financial settlement he had for the accident, after which he returned to Haiti still marveling that God had literally halted him so that he would not continue as a zombie, walking dead, but have spiritual life.

"Sometimes we are lucky enough to know that our lives have been changed, to discard the old, embrace the new, and run headlong down an immutable course..."

Jacques Yves Cousteau

WATER OF SORROWS

I think it was in July that a stranger came into the office glad to get to the mountains, away from the sweltering heat of Port-au-Prince, and commented on my sign over the door that read: AIR CONDITIONED BY MOTHER NATURE. Along with introductions, he gave me a card and explained that Jacques Cousteau and his son Jean-Michel were filming a documentary in Haiti. He asked if Jean-Michel and his crew could come interview us. Arrangements were made, and two days later we had a half-day visit and filming with Jean-Michel. We enjoyed talking with him and his team about our experiences in some of the greatest and most beautiful waters of the world.

The young Cousteau laughed as we recounted the story of our friend Cecil and the big stingray he speared. The giant ray rose to the surface and started east, taking Cecil with him as he held fast to the length of the cord which attached to his spear gun behind the ray. Cecil knew he needed help, so as he raced by with the ray in the lead, Cecil grabbed our friend Jack. All I could do was watch in wonder the unlikely display of water-skiing with the ray as the determined engine pulling Cecil who would not let go, and Jack who was the caboose. Eventually, the ray wore down and the attendees at the mission leaders' seminar enjoyed a much appreciated change of menu!

Then there was the time Ti Jo (an Arab merchant friend) was with us on the South coast. Ti Jo speared a snapper, which he laid by a big sea rock, and surfaced to reload his rubber-strap-powered spear gun. He asked Cecil to go down and get his fish by the rock. Cecil found instead a giant grouper, which sleeping looked like a rock. He speared the grouper. We helped him get it into the boat and were surprised when it spit out Ti Jo's fish. We took the fish back to the Mission to share with the mountain people who rarely got a taste of seafood.

We also shared with Cousteau and his team the conservation efforts of our sea-loving friend Robert Baussan. He developed a glass-bottomed boat, and for a period of time took tours over Iroquois Reef, home to a greater variety of coral than any other known reef as well as some of the largest sponges in the world. He successfully had the reef declared a national park, but unfortunately no park rules or controls were ever applied.

The film the Cousteaus created contained little of the information we shared during the visit at the Mission. We were able, however, to share our Christian reasons for the Mission and the part we were playing to combat the three issues highlighted in Cousteau's film *Haiti—Water of Sorrows*: deforestation, Vodou, and over-population.

He will be like a tree planted by the water
that sends out its roots by a stream.

He won't fear when the heat comes,
and his leaves will be green.

In a year of drought he won't be concerned,
nor will he stop producing fruit.

Jeremiah 17:8

TREES ON THE MOUNTAINTOP

When Wallace and I were at the Mission, farmers would say the mountains were "showing their bones" due to stony gashes in the mountainside caused by deforestation. While holding his infant son, our son, Wally, Jr., looked out onto the barren mountaintop and said, "Son, when you grow up, there will be trees on that mountaintop." With that statement the reforestation project was born. That's when Andy and Gordon of Wheaton College came to Haiti to work with Wally.

There were several challenges. One was learning how to grow the trees. Before Andy and Gordon arrived, we actually bought trailer loads of topsoil from farmers to fill little plastic bags to grow individual tree seedlings. These seedlings were relatively heavy—adults could only carry about two dozen at a time in a basket on their heads. Andy and Gordon adapted and developed a "root trainer system" that had been introduced to Haiti by a Dutch horticulturist, which made it possible to carry more tree seedlings at a time. One seed would be in one section of a narrow pocket that led young, newly-sprouting roots downward with no tangles. Opened like a book, the pockets would release the tree seedling with all its roots trained to go down and hold the soil where it was planted. A special light, artificial soil of pulverized moss and vermiculite in each pocket permitted an adult to carry 200 seedlings at a time.

Another challenge was learning what the costs were of running a nursery and finding funds to meet those costs. In order to grow the tree seedlings, we needed seeds. Our son Wally was born in Haiti and resourceful. He paid some small mountain boys to observe the time when pine cones were about to expel their tiny seeds. He had them gather into a soda bottle the seeds from the cones where they stayed safe from pests. Wally paid for the seeds by the bottle full. The young boys always left dirt around the seeds for extra volume, but Wally would clean the seeds, then measure them and pay the boys accordingly. This harvest provided adequate seeds for the nursery.

We had many local volunteers who assisted us in checking on the large amounts of seedlings being taken into the mountains for planting. Andy and Gordon trained them in how to properly care for the young trees—about watering, soils, pest control, and seasons, so that they could go out into the communities and teach others.

Trees of every sort were grown—Grevillea with fern-like leaves for shade, Neem with seeds to pound for insecticide, Guava for fragrant fruit that settles digestion, Pine, and Loquat with tiny plum-shaped fruits loved by children. In addition to these, it was felt that local Antillean Pines, which grew slowly, made the toughest lumber, and were the most likely to withstand hurricanes, should also be grown. However, multiplying the pines was not easy. We had to take small tree seedlings from below the mother tree in hopes they might grow in the nursery. A friend brought South American Chaya bush cuttings, so we also got a little grove of small Chaya trees going.

Psalm 1:3 tells us to be like "a tree planted by the rivers of water, that bringeth forth fruit in season; his leaf also shall not wither;

and whatsoever he doeth shall prosper." The Bible makes precise mention of trees 280 times and in Psalm 1 there is a promise of high dividends for investing in them. Eventually we began to see those dividends. As the idea of tree planting and the availability of tree seedlings increased, businesses and professional people began to want to get small trees on their properties. Wally ruled, "If they come in a car, they must pay ten cents per tree seedling, but if they walk in over the mountain trails with a basket, they get the trees for free." Church folks in the mountains gathered friends to meet our truck loaded with tree seedlings at the end of the road from the mission nursery. Eager people carefully gathered plastic bags of as many as they could carry in baskets on their heads. At annual church association conferences we distributed bundles of cuttings, and bushes grew in six of Haiti's ten departments.

The best fundraiser to support the reforestation project came as a result of Wally's wife, Betty, and her love of flowers. Wally wanted to grow some flowers for Betty, so he planted seeds in pots. They grew so well there were more than she needed, so he brought the excess down to the Mountain Maid Self Help Outlet. He soon learned that the city women were fighting with each other to buy the few potted flowers. A new project was born, and thousands of potted flowers have since been grown and sold, enabling the growing of millions of trees distributed free to the mountain farmers. This also gave Wally another idea: Why not grow poinsettias to sell at Christmas? Previously all potted poinsettias were imported. Wally contacted, Paul Ecky, a Christian man in California, who donated all the root cuttings for the poinsettia. The flowers would start in the nurseries months before to be beautiful and ready for sale come Christmas. Many hundreds were grown and city women competed with one another to see who had them first to decorate their homes. This project not only brought the funds needed to support the reforestation project for the year, it also helped spread the concept of decorating for Christmas.

Gordon and Andy soon realized that it was time to cash in on their investment of learning to work with simple people. The investment paid off. Andy moved on to get a master's degree in Auburn, Alabama. He spent the next thirty years with an organization in Ethiopia that eventually included Haiti in its outreach. Gordon moved toward studying languages and a life of Bible translation in Africa with Wycliffe. He eventually became a board member of the same organization in which he invested. How is that for a long-time dividend?

During those busy years, the effect of our investment in trees continued to spread in spite of droughts, continued charcoal production, saplings harvested for building poles, landslides, and destruction caused by hungry animals. The tree nursery grew and expanded until it was producing over 500,000 tree seedlings a year. Wally kept his promise to his son. A mountain once eroded and gravelly is now entirely terraced with green gardens and little masonry homes showing through lush yards of trees, bamboo, and bananas.

His Lamps

His lamps we are,
To shine where He shall say:
And lamps are not for sunny rooms,
Nor for the light of day;

But for the dark places of the earth,
Where shame and wrong and crime have birth,
Or for the murky twilight grey,
Where wandering sheep have gone astray,

Or where the Lamp of Faith grows dim,
And souls are groping after Him.
And as sometimes a flame we find,
Clear-shining through the night,

So dark we do not see the lamp
But only see the Light,
So may we shine, His love the flame,
That men may glorify His Name.

Annie Johnson Flint

SELF-HELP

When I think of the humble beginnings of our Self Help Project, I think of May. I do not remember which of her five children she had with her the first time she passed by the Mission on the Kenscoff Road, but I do remember her sincere graciousness as we enjoyed a cup of traditional herb tea together. I showed her a few simple aprons and course cotton tea napkins made by some mountain women we were helping to begin the Self Help Project. The items were obviously the work of beginners, but May showed a genuine interest in the project and appreciated them. She purchased several. When I later learned that her husband, David, was with the US Embassy in Port-au-Prince, I realized that it was not because of the low price that May bought the items; she wanted to help.

As we got to know Dave and May, we realized they were different from other U.S. State Department Officials—they were more like missionaries than diplomats. They not only understood the importance of working to make things happen, they also recognized the connection between happiness and usefulness, production and prosperity. They taught their children to participate, to learn by doing, and the relationship between faith and works. They came alongside us to support the Self Help

Project, which was an entirely new concept in Haiti. May not only continued to come to the Mission to buy the items made by the local women, but she also brought all of her visitors and friends from the diplomatic and international communities. The mountain women soon realized that whenever the big black car with CONSULAT on the license plate came to the Mission, they would make enough money that day to buy some oil, rice, and beans for their children.

May became the voluntary creative director for the Self Help Project. She made suggestions of more marketable designs and products while providing public relations and outreach. May's zeal was contagious, and interest spread rapidly. The mountain women were enthusiastic and grateful to be earning money to help with their ever-increasing families. Soon tourist drivers were bringing visitors to buy aprons, placemats, napkins, and other items. The mountain women worked hard to improve their work, more women asked to learn, and even men asked to be part of the project and learned their own style of coarser embroidery. Gradually the project built up a modest inventory.

The only place to receive May and her friends was in the living room of the mission house—our home. The living room was warm and friendly with soft cream-colored, irregular masonry walls, a large stone fireplace, and a yellow and brown tile floor. There were wide picture windows that gave an awesome, sweeping view of the steep mountains directly across the ravine. We could see the farmers' little huts and hear the echo of their drums, which were used both for dancing and Vodou worship. We also would hear the sound of the conch shell blown by the mountain crier in staccato-like code to spread news from village to village.

When visitors came to the Mission, almost everyone asked to use our restroom since there were no rest stops outside of the city. Offering our guests a cup of herbal tea became an opportunity for conversation. Many people wanted to know more about the Self

Help Project, the Mission, and us. This often led to people reflecting on their own lives and learning more about themselves and recognizing their need to know God. We told them the Bible teaches that "this is eternal life, that they may know...the only true God, and Jesus Christ" (John 17:3).

It soon became obvious that our living room was insufficient to host so many visitors, and I remember saying to May one day, "I wish we might someday make a little tea room on the road in front of the Mission where people could stop for physical and spiritual refreshment and buy the self-help items. Perhaps we could hang a banner marked TEA AND TOILETS across the road from the Mission!" We both laughed. But the idea caught both of our imaginations, and we waited for God's timing.

Meanwhile, May offered her Jeep with a winch to help some men from the Mission preserve the tumbling-down fort not far off the Kenscoff Road. The six-foot-deep stone walls of Fort Jacques, built between 1807-1810, were caving in from water seepage.

One of the first things was to clean off the shrubbery and growth that was destroying the fort. Then the men made a stone and dirt ramp outside to move a cannon back inside to the firing sites of the upper terrace. May operated her Jeep winch to drag the one ton, 18th Century cast-iron French cannon up the ramp and into the fort. The largest cannon at the fort was the only one that had been cast with the royal crest of King George III of England.

Wallace had wisely seen that expressing an interest in preserving the fort was also a declaration of the Mission's concern and interest in the history of Haiti; this gave him and the other people from the Mission an opportunity to work with the local people and share the Gospel in ways other than from the pulpit. The local Vodou leader joined the workforce and old Julien Altidor, the only one living who remembered when the fort was still occupied, came often to inspect the clean-up work and tell stories of how General Hudicourt was the last to live in the fort with soldiers. He told us about the *tremblement de terre*, or earthquake, that broke up the one-hundred-year-old timbers and caused the slate roof over the inner court of the fort to collapse. There were still many pieces of broken slate to verify Julien's story. We still have a picture we took with a little box camera of us standing in the doorway of the high-peaked, solid stone old powder house that stood a few yards from the fort before it collapsed.

May found a metal detector and volunteered her son Bobby to help us find and sort metal objects around the fort while on summer vacation from college. Before making drains and sealing the top rampant with cement, it was important to salvage and classify all the metal items. May kept Bobby and her daughter Linda busy all summer locating, digging out, cleaning, and classifying two hundred pounds of shrapnel, bullets, old coins, uniform buttons, etc. It was fun, but it was also disciplined, hard work, which May, along with her son and daughter, embraced with the attitude, "If a job is worth doing, it is worth doing well."

During that summer while working with us, May hadn't forgotten the Self Help Project, and on December 23 we received a wonderful surprise. The Mission was hosting their annual pre-Christmas party for foreign missionaries and representatives of other Non-Governmental Organizations. The party always offered lots of special foods, encouragement, inspiration and the message that "God so loved the world that He gave His only Son" (John 3:16). Giving gifts was not traditional, but May came with Linda for a brief visit and gave us a lovely Christmas card, a letter, and a check designated for the construction of "tea and toilet" building. Wow! God had provided in his time.

Soon after, Dave resigned from the State Department, and the family left Haiti. They continued to help Haiti by sending support for children to attend school at the Mission. They settled in Wyoming where they took up the challenge of ranching and sent us pictures of their herds of buffalo, as well as of them pitching hay and checking irrigation ditches, along with news of their children. We saw Bobby once after he finished his studies in geology. It was easier for us to relate to his commitment to water in the Denver Basin and his travels to Bolivia for geological research than to his study and passion for dinosaur footprints in the western United States! When we learned that he became Bob after his Bobby was born, we recalled his attention and gentle concern for the children of the mountains of Haiti. When told that one of Linda's sculptures is on display in a museum, I recalled the exercise of her patience and creativity while in Haiti.

Having lived in other parts of the world, May was the sort of person to find purpose wherever she might be. Although they did not remain in Haiti, I think May knew that she had been sent as a link. I doubt that she ever imagined the many links that would make up the chain and its strength, nor where the chain would lead.

My Name Is I AM

"When you live in the past,
with its mistakes and regrets,
it is hard.
I am not there.
My name is not I WAS.

When you live in the future,
with its problems and fears,
it is hard.
I am not there.
My name is not I WILL BE.

When you live in this moment,
It is not hard.
I am here.
My name is I AM."

Helen Mallicoat

UNCHARTED SEAS

Thanks to May's family we had the funds to build the tea room. Now we needed the right people to design, build, and finish it. Alone in an old storeroom, I was sorting used clothing in the securely-packed missionary barrel when, upon straightening from the back-breaking job, I was shocked to see a foreign man watching me. Recognition dawned and surprised, I exclaimed, "Gary what in the world are you doing here? How did you get 4,500 feet up the mountain and find us here at Fermathe?"

You see, I expected Gary to be in Florida. He had proudly shown us a marvelous sailboat he had crafted. I remember our high admiration for Gary as we heard how he had weathered storms. One, in particular, had left him for five days on rough, uncharted, open seas floating alone without a radio or any contact. We quickly learned that Gary was not only an amazing craftsman and seaman, but he was also a devout man of God. We sensed the love and prayers of his Dutch parents for their only child. We had promised to pray for each other, and we went back to Haiti hoping that someday Haiti might have such clever, skilled workmen.

Now, Gary stood before me in his quiet way, half-smiling, "You would ask me what I am doing here...Well, to be truthful, I am here because I am fleeing from evil." So there, while standing in the warehouse, Gary told me his circumstances.

His wife had left him for someone with more money, and he was finding that life in Florida for a single, handsome man was a pathway to evil. There were many young, pretty women who were aggressively looking for someone, but Gary thought it was best just to get out. God brought the Mission to mind. Indeed, Gary was sent to us!

At that time the Mission house had a broken wall and no one had the knowledge or skills to patch it. With gentle modesty, Gary smiled and suggested, "Maybe I can try to fix it using some chicken wire and mortar." Gary quickly put his talents to work, and soon the wall looked better than new.

Gary also wanted to learn Creole. He asked for a copy of the *How to Learn Creole* book, and it was a common sight every morning to see Gary sitting with the essential cup of strong, black Haitian coffee studying his language book. Then he would go to work teaching the local workers new and better ways to build at a level of expertise then unknown to the mountain people.

Weeks later this skilled, quiet, gentle man approached us saying he wished to tell us about a woman in Florida named Gail that he admired but had not proposed to because she was not a born again believer in Christ. He knew his parents would have discouraged any serious friendship, so he took thoughtful walks and prayed for her salvation. How much he prayed, I could never guess. What I do know is one day Gary came to us like a brave, frightened man and presented a plan.

"I want to tell you something. I would like to invite Gail to come stay at the Mission a few days. I know I cannot marry her because she is not a Christian… not yet. Perhaps she should come to Haiti and visit you folks and experience more of the Christian faith and our friendship together."

Wallace and I thought that was a reasonable request, so plans were suggested and made, and the invitation for Gail to visit the Mission was sent via post.

Although I cannot recall all the details, I remember that we loved Gary and felt frightened for him. We selfishly assumed that there could be no one "good enough" for him. I also remember two months later, the shame I felt for assuming we would help Gail make the decision to become a Christian when Gary shared the miraculous story of how Gail had accepted Christ.

God had wonderfully answered his prayer in a most unusual way. Gail went to a dentist with a toothache, but when she arrived, the office was closed with no explanation, so she went to a different dentist nearby. When she met the new dentist, casual greetings quickly turned into a conversation about faith. That day Gail experienced 1 John 5:20: "And we know that the Son of God has come and has given us an understanding, that we may know Him who is true; and we are in Him who is true, in His Son Jesus Christ. This is the true God and eternal life." Gail was quick to share her newfound joy with Gary who understood God was at work to do "His will according to His good pleasure" (Ephesians 1:5).

Gail did come to Haiti. For us, her visit was much too short, but for them, it was just right. It was enough time for them to order wedding rings from a Haitian goldsmith and have the Mission's blessing on their union. Then the happy couple returned to Florida for their wedding.

During this time, we had purchased the materials to make the tea room for the Mountain Maid Self Help Outlet where the items made in the self-help program would be sold. Now we needed someone to install the heavy glass fronts and use the rustic boards to create lounges in front of the large stone fireplace as reading, meditation, and rest areas for visitors. God had clearly sent Gary for this purpose. The Mountain Maid Outlet became Haiti's number one mountain retreat where the great mountainside overlook reminds us of Psalm 121: 1-2. "I lift up my eyes toward the mountains—from where will my help come? My help is from the Lord, maker of heaven and earth."

After Gary and Gail were married and had been living in Florida, Gary's expertise was called upon again when interested people asked Wallace and me about finding a source of fuel that could be used in firing ceramics. Remembering that Gary had helped Gail's successful ceramic business, making thousands and thousands of thimbles, we thought he might just know something about kilns. We explained to him that wood, electricity, or gas would not be available, although we did have enough bricks to build a six-foot kiln. But that left the giant question of what could be used to fire it! So Gary came, not to flee from evil as before, but to make a new kind of kiln that would run on used car oil and water. The tall chimney would forcefully draw the heat across the chamber as the mixture of used oil and water would drip onto the preheated plate. Once again God met a need in the unlikeliness of ways, yet another announcement that little is much when God is in it!

May God grant you always…
A sunbeam to warm you,
A moonbeam to charm you
A sheltering Angel
so nothing can harm you.
Laughter to cheer you.
Faithful friends near you.
And whenever you pray,
Heaven to hear you.

An Irish Blessing

MY HELP IS FROM THE LORD

With the growing popularity of the Mountain Maid Self Help Outlet, many tourists started coming to the Mission on the Kenscoff Road. Visiting dignitaries also made a point to visit. I remember one year when President Tolbert of Liberia and his wife were on an official visit to Haiti. A Haitian army officer and the Secretary of the Liberian Embassy came with Madame Tolbert's agenda, explaining that she and her entourage planned to visit the Mission the following Friday. Madame Tolbert planned to shop at the Mountain Maid Self Help Outlet and visit with Wallace and me.

We had met President and Madame Tolbert when he was president of the Baptist World Alliance and knew they were professing Christians. We looked forward to Madame's visit on Friday morning as a time of Christian fellowship. We were surprised to see her arrive with three carloads of formally dressed and heavily armed Liberian and Haitian military officers.

As Madame Tolbert, her secretary, and her Haitian hostess stopped just inside the entrance of our home, she was startled by two of our decorations—deep pink, stuffed flamingos. They looked so real that Madame reached out and touched their waxy bills. She then turned to her aid beside her and said, "Get me two like that to take to Liberia." The Haitian man shot me a questioning look, then replied to her, "*Mais oui*, Madame." I knew, however, that she was asking the impossible.

Years ago, when our sons were younger, they would go bird hunting at a nearby lake, Etang Saumatre. Canadian ducks often found refuge in the lake and nearby reed beds where flocks of flamingos searched in the water for food. After one hunting trip, in particular, one of our sons and his friend returned with two full gunny sacks, two pellet guns, and a shotgun. When they untied their gunny sacks and emptied the contents on the table, we expected to see ducks. Imagine our horror when we saw four dead flamingoes. The boys were instantly defensive, "It's not our fault! We decided to bring Mom a beautiful surprise of one flamingo to have stuffed. The others were all a mistake!"

We felt like partners in crime as we cleaned the two most battered ones, not for proper burial, which seemed the most appropriate way to dispose of such beautiful creatures, but for the stew pot. Dressed down, those beautiful flamingos were pretty scrawny. The two other birds had to be kept cool while we looked for a taxidermist. There was no listing, no addresses, no street names, and certainly no phone numbers. Long before we were able to search for things we needed on the Internet or call on a cell phone, we had another effective means of searching—word of mouth. So we started asking if anyone knew of a taxidermist.

"Yes, someone had heard of someone."

"Yes, there was one, but he must be old by now."

I think it was Brother Simone who finally found the taxidermist, Mr. Whiteman, who told us he had learned the trade from his deceased father. While he was advanced in years, he told us he certainly was not too old to still follow the trade. He also was the one who told us killing flamingos was illegal, and he was putting himself at risk working on them, as he could be subject to prosecution. However, the price was right, and he was still willing to stuff the birds. He did a good job, and they looked beautiful standing straight and tall with their necks and head in a natural position. Many people had admired them over the years, and now they had caught the eye of the First Lady of Liberia.

Madame Tolbert was a sister in Christ, so our visit with her was easy and encouraging. She was happy to hear about the growth and influence of evangelism in rural Haiti. She told me about the death of her grown daughter, and I told her how our youngest of three sons, David, died at the age of twenty-six in a scuba diving accident. We shared our experiences of trust in the absolute sovereignty of God and both felt enriched by a time of Christian closeness. She wanted to know more about the Mission's outreach, specifically the Self Help Project as it taught skills to the rural population and met an economic need. She invited me to go to Liberia in hopes that together we might launch a similar effort for the women in the villages there.

Later, while Madame and her secretary shopped in the Mountain Maid Self Help Outlet, a very worried Haitian military officer took me aside and asked me where—how—to get the pink flamingos for the First Lady of Liberia. My mind raced... would I have to tell him? If I did, I would be telling a Haitian military officer that we had illegally killed flamingos. I realized the Mission was caught with its pants down!

I mentioned a couple of places he might try, but he got the vibe that I didn't want to talk about the subject anymore and left. I thought I was rid of him until he returned the next day with the chief of the department of Haitian tourism and government protocol. This is it, I thought to myself. Imagine my relief when the chief offered to buy one of the flamingos for Madame Tolbert! Her aid had it packed and shipped to Liberia, and the other flamingo remains in the museum at the Mission.

The More You Give

The more you give, the more you get.
The more you laugh, the less you fret.
The more you do unselfishly,
the more you live abundantly.
The more of everything you share,
the more you'll always have to spare.
The more you love, the more you'll find
that life is good and friends are kind.
For only what we give away,
enriches us from day to day.

Author Unknown

YEP!
MOVING RIGHT ALONG!

For many years Port-au-Prince, Haiti was used as a port of rest and relaxation for employees and personnel from the U.S. Naval base in Guantanamo Bay (Gitmo), Cuba. Each Thursday in the early morning Navy planes transported pre-registered passengers from Gitmo to Port-au-Prince. The plane returned immediately with U.S. Embassy passengers from Port-au-Prince who would spend the day on base shopping at the commissaries and getting medical and dental care. In the late afternoon, the plane would return the U.S. Embassy passengers to Haiti and pick up the Gitmo passengers who had enjoyed what they called, "the Haiti experience."

This service schedule continued for many years between Gitmo and Haiti. The Gitmo people disliked the hassle of over-zealous vendors, beggars, and pickpockets in Port-au-Prince, and they were glad to learn that the U.S. Embassy not only approved but recommended the Mountain Maid Gift Shop at the Mission fifteen miles north of Port-au-Prince on the Kenscoff Road. The quiet, orderly friendliness of the Mountain Maid Self Help Outlet, plus the kindness of coffee or tea with one of Granny's homemade sweets, made the shop a necessary stop for many from Gitmo.

We old-timers tried to make a few hours available each Thursday to visit with the Gitmo folks who often had questions about Haiti, the Mission and desired to talk about other personal issues that made them welcome a compassionate listening ear.

It was with this backdrop that we met Mary Todd. She separated herself from a group of several other ladies from Gitmo to introduce herself. "I am visiting my son who is a Naval officer in Gitmo. My name is Mary Todd, but not the one married to Abraham Lincoln!" That was the first time I heard this phrase that would become one of her signatures. We enjoyed our conversation with this lively, attractive lady with her sequined-covered sandals, bright red manicured toes, and over-sized dangling earrings. At the end of her visit, we exchanged addresses to keep in touch.

Two weeks later we received a letter from Mary asking we write back if we thought there might be a place for her at the Mission. We felt prompted to reply, yes, and remembering that she was a retired schoolteacher, suggested she teach English at the local high school the following semester.

In addition to being a retired schoolteacher, Mary was also a fine musician. She was a beautiful woman who into her eighties, showed many of her drum major and college days' "beauty queen" attributes. She had a happy laugh, made straight-forward comments, and was honest without niceties. Her commitment to Bible truths, full of tales about her grandfather Pastor Beachman's horseback circuit-preaching of hard, close-cut theology left no reason to wonder why Mary was at the Mission. She considered "tolerance" as sin, and had no patience with "liberalism" that made her exclaim, "Balderdash!"

She loved to tell about her South Carolina ancestry and fascinated us with reports of visits to her nine living aunts and uncles ages eighty to ninety-three years. Mary was a favorite with those who passed by as well as the local population who knew her as "Miz Merie."

Mary Lynn Todd became such a part of the Mission on the Kenscoff Road that many thought she was my blood sister. On rare occasions, she and I would go to Port-au-Prince together. She always had too much to do—preparing lessons, teaching music, organizing staff dinners, decorating for special events, the list goes on and on. She also had discovered that going to Port-au-Prince with me wasn't usually fun for her as it meant fighting city traffic, waiting to see the director of some department, and suffering in the tropical heat that soon turned her beautiful curly white hair into sweaty strings.

There was one special trip, however, where we went to town together. Mary needed a few personal items that could only be found in the crowded market streets. Together we worked our way through the masses of people. Taking care to avoid all kinds of street nastiness and yet scarcely able to see ahead through the crowd, we saw two street merchants staring at us as we approached. We caught their conversation as we passed… "No! No, that is not what makes them have all those white-people wrinkles…it is the kind of cosmetics they used when they were young!"

Mary and I never let on that we heard and understood them. Shall I say we agreed together to change our cosmetics! Truly with all our white hair, our lean, willowy bodies, our agile high stepping, as well as our skin wrinkles, termed by the local people as "pleats," we could have been sisters. The truth is that I was flattered by such a comparison until one day when we were together we met a stranger who said, "Wow! Two nice women!" and then turning directly to Mary he continued, "I can tell that in your day you were quite a looker, eh?"

Volunteers came and went, but Mary stayed, becoming discouraged only rarely when she would complain, "I seem to be getting poor press." Since Mary had been a teacher her whole life, she often spoke very directly. Visitors sometimes thought she came off too bossy: "Hey, did you forget that I told you to wait in line?" "No one is to come in that kitchen door—don't you know there is a dining room door?—so please go out and this time, be sure to come in the dining room door." "Did no one ever tell you it is improper to wear your cap inside?" Whenever things got tense, or people's feelings were sensitive, Mary would simply say, "Yep! But moving right along..." and the whole atmosphere would change. That eventually became the peace treaty. "Yep! Moving right along!"

The longest it ever took Mary to bounce back was the time her fabulous double diamond dinner ring disappeared when workmen repaired her apartment. We all felt the loss of something we had appreciated and enjoyed. Eventually, Mary simply said, "Yep, now moving right along..."

We all enjoyed Mary's music—she was the best piano player ever—there were no lyrics, none, that she did not know—old ones, new ones, church, party, radio, concert, or whatever! The only question was how to keep Mary from jazzing them until no one could keep up and everyone ended in hilarious, jolly laughter.

She became "Miz Merie" to the high and the low of Haiti and almost never "Madame Todd." Her ex-primary school students from South Carolina felt close enough to call her "Mrs. Toad" and sent her gifts of various frog souvenirs—most of them glass, metal, or ceramic. Mary was the type of person one never forgets, and we are so glad she was one of those who passed by the Mission on the Kenscoff Road.

In Jesus

I've tried in vain a thousand ways
My fears to quell, my hopes to raise;
But what I need, the Bible says,
Is ever, only Jesus.

My soul is night, my heart is steel
I cannot see, I cannot feel;
For light, for life, I must appeal
In simple faith to Jesus.

He died, He lives, He reigns, He pleads;
There's love in all His words and deeds;
There's all a guilty sinner needs
Forevermore in Jesus.

Tho' some should sneer, and some should blame,
I'll go with all my guilt and shame;
I'll go to Him because His Name,
Above all names, is Jesus.

James Procter

MILICENT'S REFUGE

In addition to coming to the Mission to visit the Mountain Maid Self Help Outlet, many came to enjoy the cooler temperatures of the mountains and recuperate—body, mind, and soul. Milicent was one of these, saying, "I came just so I can be alone with myself and sometimes with God."

Milicent was a nurse volunteer working in the hospital in Limbe, another part of Haiti. I remember the one time I delivered a small jar of Granny's special wild strawberry jam as an excuse to infringe on her solitude. I was surprised when this frail-looking, genteel, quiet little blond nurse insisted I stay with her to talk. I soon learned more about her past. She had worked in a hospital in China as a nurse caring for people who were violently mistreated by the Mao revolutionaries. She told me of assisting surgeries and amputations without general anesthesia. More than once she did the post-operative, nursing soldiers who sat up eating with no sedative the first day after the amputations. She greatly admired the older generation of stalwart, mind-over-matter Chinese. The admiration and pride she felt for the Chinese people seemed to have become part of her own emotional and psychological self.

When the patients learned that Milicent spoke Chinese, they began telling her stories of how the Communists were destroying anything that was old: paintings, sculptures, books. With quiet emotion, Milicent told how an old Chinese individual would bring her a chosen piece in the night asking her, "Please keep this. It is valuable and will be destroyed if you do not take it." As the revolution became more violent and expanded, the time for all Westerners to leave closed in. Even on Milicent's way to the airport, Chinese people kept bringing her more priceless art asking her, "Please save it." Airport security seized all of the items from Milicent when she arrived and usually they would have been destroyed. Miraculously, the airport inspectors eventually gave all the items back to her and said she could keep them since "she didn't have fire in her eyes like the other foreigners."

Milicent came to the Mission three times. Each time she came, she brought a fine, valued piece of very old Chinese art as a gift. There was the over seven-hundred-year-old high relief, engraved stone plaque, the over four hundred-year-old carving of the Chinese sage with his sandals dangling from his staff well above the old one's balding head. The third escapes my memory, but might be the miniature carved ivory little boy with his goat that we shelter on our living room shelf.

After Milicent's horrible experiences during Mao's revolutionary China and living with the constant fear and insecurity of Haiti's dictator Papa Doc Duvalier and the Tonton Macouts, she redirected her life and became a nun as a way to pursue her life's calling of serving others.

He has told you, O man, what is good;
and what does the Lord require of you
but to do justice, and to love kindness
and to walk humbly with your God?

Micah 6:8

WASH AND CLEAN

Another couple whose life's calling was serving others, was Dr. William Larimer Mellon and his wife, Gwen. While Larimer finished his doctorate in the United States, Gwen came to Haiti and supervised the construction of Hôpital Albert Schweitzer (HAS), which opened June 26, 1956. The need was great. A healthy doctor to population ratio is 1:2,000. In the Artibonite Valley ninety miles northwest of Port-au-Prince where HAS was located, there were no doctors for the 185,000 people who lived there.

There had been a devastating hurricane and Gwen had heard that scores of starving, malnourished children were finding refuge at the Mission on the Kenscoff Road. Gwen had come to help.

When she woke the next morning she entered the room with a bright," Good morning!" and asked, "Please tell me the story of those big, old, hand-hewn boards in the magnificent ceiling in my room!"

Actually, I thought to myself, they were ugly, patched over with masking tape and painted with cheap water paint we'd put there to keep scorpions, termites' dust, and even rats from falling onto the bed, but we didn't tell Gwen any of that. The ceiling was "magnificent" to Gwen because she saw beauty and wonder in everything. So we told her how the boards had been ballast on a sailing vessel from Germany a century ago when the ships were sent to Haiti for Campeche dye wood.

Gwen had seen the best, the most, and the unusual of everything great and grand, and now she would see the depravity of poverty. She was ready to go to work to help with the children, but where should we put her? In records? There were no parents to give names, ages, and addresses for the children. Should she weigh the children? Most of them were too weak and limp for that. How about feeding them? They certainly needed to eat, but because of excessive diarrhea, even that job was complicated! Maybe we could send her to the clinic to help with the less-extreme cases.

At the clinic, Gwen saw an elderly missionary woman washing the diarrhea-filled bedding and clothing of the children. There were no disposables in the mountains of Haiti—only torn up sheets which had to be reused many times. Gwen sent the elderly missionary woman to do other things and appointed herself as chief of clean-up and washing for the children.

It was not the nicest nor the easiest task. Soap had to be cut up and melted, and water was only available as mountain women arrived with five gallons in containers on their heads. Water was heated over charcoal. Everything had to be spread out in the open under the tropical sun for drying and disinfecting. It was a never-ending task as all day more and more changes were necessary. Gwen never complained, but she did ask the elderly missionary for suggestions about suppressing the odor and happily followed the suggestion to smolder some dry citronella and roots, using whiffs of the smoke as a deoderizer.

Thus began our friendship with the Mellons and the relationship between the Mission and HAS. Once when Dr. Mellon was visiting the Mission, he told us he had once asked his famous grandmother, "What is the greatest thing in the world that a man can do?" She replied, "Be a medical missionary."

Despite that advice, Larimer followed the family business and became a banker, but eventually he thought, "There must be something more in life than money." He bought a ranch and there he met and married Gwen Grant. Their life was full but not necessarily fulfilling. Dr. Mellon didn't realize that until he read an article in Life magazine about the Albert Schweitzer Hospital in Gabon, Africa. It set him to thinking. Then one day he blurted out, "I think I'll become a doctor and practice in the undeveloped world." Both Larimer and Gwen enrolled at Tulane University and decided to build their hospital in Haiti in the village of Deschapelles.

The hospital reached out to the community as a living example of Galatians 5:14, "You must love your neighbor as yourself." As Dr. Melon grew older and experienced life with his neighbors, the very poor rice farmers of the Artibonite valley, he saw that they were hungry. He found that eighty percent of their sickness was the result of malnutrition. He discovered that food production was more necessary for good health than the treatment of malnutrition and related illnesses. As he gave more of his time to his neighbors' farm production, he requested that he not be addressed as "Doctor Mellon." One would often see him wearing his old straw hat inspecting irrigation ditches in his little Willys jeep, checking the water supply and considering production problems. Even before Dr. Melon died, an Artibonite farmer told me, "We will always remember Dr. Mellon, not as a doctor, but as the good man who would stop his jeep, get out, move any large rock off the little dirt road, get back in his jeep and go on."

I remember once when we were sharing our own Christian experience and firmness of faith in Jesus—the Way, the Truth, and the Life. Dr. Melon told us, "At a certain age, I had a similar spiritual experience which has given me much peace." As he grew older the confidence and certitude of his Christian faith expressed itself in the fruits of the Spirit: love, joy, peace, patience, kindness, goodness, gentleness, and self-control, in great humility.

Dr. and Mrs. Mellon lived in a comfortable bungalow they built near the hospital. The day we stood by his grave in the shade of the big banyan tree near their house, I reflected how through their friendship and example our own lives had been enriched. I felt the challenge of the life of a humble, good man. Less than four years later, Gwen was buried beside him. I smiled when I remembered the first time she came to the Mission on the Kenscoff Road to "wash and clean."

Lean Hard

Child of My love, lean hard,
And let Me feel the pressure of your care;
I know your burden, child, I shaped it;
Balanced it in My own hand; made no proportion
In its weight to your unaided strength,
For even as I laid it on, I said,
"I will be near, and while she leans on Me,
This burden will be Mine, not hers;
So will I keep My child within the circling arms
Of My own love." Here lay it down, nor fear
To impose it on a shoulder that upholds
The government of worlds. Yet closer come:
You are not near enough. I would embrace your care;
So I might feel My child reclining on My breast.
You love Me, I know. So then do not doubt;
But, loving Me, lean hard.

May Prentiss Smith

COME IN THE DOOR

O nce Hôpital Albert Schweitzer opened, many doctors and nurses from around the world volunteered their professional help. Many found transportation to visit the Mission on the Kenscoff Road as a respite from the stress associated with working at the overcrowded hospital. That's how we met the young Christian doctor named Robert (Bob). He asked if he might stay and asked if his friend Cornelia, who was coming from Radcliff College, might stay as well.

Tall, pretty Cornelia arrived and soon became "Cornie" as we all sat around the stone fireplace keeping warm from the damp mountain evening. We learned that Cornie grew up in a devout Unitarian family. Her parents felt they had fulfilled their duty to their beautiful and unusually bright daughter by sending her to the Ivy League College. The first time she was exposed to the Christian faith was when John Scott was a guest speaker at Radcliff.

"I knew that my relationship to God was important," Cornie said. "Actually, since childhood, my relationship with the Heavenly Father had grown to be the thing I most enjoyed. I awakened each morning eager to talk to the Father, and through the years, I learned to listen to Him, which really became a meaningful conversation for me. My roommate also had daily exchanges with God, but I soon realized that she listened to Him by reading her Bible. She would exclaim over certain marvels as she read, and she would humbly bow in self-humiliation when she talked to Him. She spoke of repentance, forgiveness, and grace.

"We often read the Bible together and talked about how a person can know and enjoy God. One day as I read the Bible by myself, I looked upward in anticipation of an encounter with God. He said to me, 'Cornie, I have often talked with you from the window of heaven, but I must tell you that I cannot continue to meet with you from the window.' I was startled and frightened as I told him how much these times together meant to me. Almost weeping I told him, 'Father, I cannot live if I can't meet with You. Meeting with You is the most important thing in my life.' He answered, 'Cornie, I know you like it, but this is only a partial meeting. To really meet with Me, you must go around and come in the door and talk with me from the inside.'

"I was unable to understand what he meant by 'come in the door.' Although frightened, I was determined that whatever the cost, I would not lose the wonder of being able to meet with Him. In my mind's eye, I decided to walk away from the window position and move around to the other side where I saw a big open door leading to the Father's throne room. Remembering that He said, 'You must come through the door and be inside to talk to me,' I stepped inside, looking down the long corridor toward the throne room. I was walking on the long, red carpet that covered the floor leading the way to the throne—to the Father. There was One standing beside Him who smiled as He nodded to me saying, "Come."

Per Bob's plan, I eventually steered the conversation to the topic of relationships. We talked about how a mutual commitment to Christ is important for long-term happiness and how together they would have to agree on church affiliation, child-rearing, and tithing. Everything seemed to be going well until I mentioned tithing. Imagine my chagrin when Cornie quietly asked, "What about tithing—I don't think I understand." Bob and I explained how a tenth of the income we receive belongs to the Lord and should be given to Him. Still uncertain, Cornie asked, "But how is that? I thought that when I became a Christian, everything, including myself, belongs to Him." She was right, of course! Sitting on a low stool in front of the cheerful fire, I humbly bowed my head, ashamed but amazed how this new Christian had out-raced me in my own Christian thinking.

It was a memorable weekend for Cornie and Bob, and later they married and lived happily ever after. I sometimes shared Cornie's story with other young people struggling to find their way to the Father, searching to reach the Father but by-passing the Savior, "the way, the truth, and the life" (John 14:6).

Follow Me

Follow me, and I will make you…
Make you speak My words with power;
Make you channels of My mercy;
Make you helpful every hour.

Follow Me, and I will make you…
Make you what you cannot be;
Make you loving, trustful, godly;
Make you even like to Me.

L. S. P.

TALK-TO-DO

Warren and Gretchen were among our favorites of those who passed by the Mission on the Kenscoff Road. In those days, we knew that our friends were highly professional, extraordinary people, but we had no idea that through spiritual truth, academic excellence, and fearless research they would become world-famous. They served as associate professors of Harvard's School of Public Health and were recipients of numerous awards including the Donald McKay Medal of the American Society of Tropical Medicine, the International Health Award from Mother Theresa, the HSPH Alumni Award of Merit from Harvard University, and a Presidential citation from Bill Clinton. When they came to the Mission, they brought friends to visit or multinational students from the Harvard School of Public Health. Sometimes they came to find spiritual courage and rest. Other times we sent for them asking for their help. Whatever the reason, we were always glad they came.

As young graduates from the Medical School of Nebraska, the couple answered the call of missions and began their work in Kimpese, Congo, until in the midst of political strife, they had to be taken by helicopter to safety. In the 1960s they studied and worked at the Harvard School of Public Health before taking positions at Hôpital Albert Schweitzer. Their first year there the hospital saw 650 children with tetanus, 550 of them newborns. Warren and Gretchen knew neonatal tetanus should not be taking these lives since there was a vaccine for the disease. But they also recognized how difficult it was to reach the rural population of Haiti with vaccines and recruit the staff to give them. So they created a unique plan that brought them renown and would be duplicated around the world. They brought the vaccines to the people. On market day, they would arrive before the market opened and would talk with the merchants. They would explain why they were there and set up an outdoor clinic. On at least one morning, their small team of workers gave 8,000 inoculations. The Community Health Program was a success. Today, it's been years since the hospital has seen a case of tetanus, even though the population in the area is now over three times larger than the 70,000 it served when Warren and Gretchen began.

Yet, for all of their medical accomplishments, Warren and Gretchen were quick to point out that more important than all their awards was the knowledge that their names were written in the Lamb's Book of Life. They never talked about themselves, but we all saw that their "talk-to-do" ratio was very high. We sought their advice on ways to improve the Mission on the Kenscoff Road and create a program reduced in size and cost for the mountain areas of West Haiti. Perhaps this collaboration, along with the more meaningful "missionary echo in their hearts" was the reason that through the years they continued to be among the favorites of "those who passed by" the Mission on the Kenscoff Road. Is there a saying "once a missionary—always a missionary?" If there isn't, there should be. Didn't Saint Paul write to the Romans "for the gifts and the calling of God are irrevocable" (Romans 11:29) and we join with Warren and Gretchen in answering, "My life is my argument."

Let your speech always be gracious, seasoned with salt, so that you may know how you ought to answer each person.

Colossians 4:6

WALK HUMBLY
WITH YOUR GOD

Francisca worked with Warren and Gretchen on the Community Health Program at HAS and came to the Mission for a respite. During World War II, Francisca had been a nurse at a hospital on an island called Java, then part of the Netherlands East Indies, now Indonesia. In March of 1942, the Japanese Empire invaded and drove all the personnel out of the hospital at the end of pointed bamboo spears. She, along with all the other refugees, was put on a boat and sent to Suez, Egypt. In Suez, they were given a small packet of toiletries (toothbrush, comb, etc.) and from there they were sent to Europe for the duration of the war.

Francisca traveled on to Lambarene, in western Gabon, Africa where she worked and served at the hospital with Dr. Albert Schweitzer until he died in 1965. From there she came to serve at HAS in Haiti. Through her experiences, Francisca realized that her life's meaning was found in divine service to God and people and that only the Jesus of Christianity had "come that they may have life, and have it abundantly" (John 10:10).

Throughout the years, Francisca brought an appreciated quiet and oriental insight and kindness whenever she came. Once she brought a gift of the magnifying glass which Dr. Schweitzer had used every morning when he gathered the hospital staff and read the Scripture. She explained that when Dr. Schweitzer died, the staff was given the opportunity to choose any Dr. Schweitzer souvenir, and having come to love the Scriptures which had brought the light and life to her, she had chosen his magnifying glass.

Fluent in Creole and quite natural in the Haitian culture, Francisca lived very frugally so that she could pay tuition for a family of three orphan boys. When she was almost eighty, she was discouraged, tired, and fragile. She came to us and asked if she could help in the plant nursery and live at the Mission. She continued her frugal lifestyle and helped buy materials which Wallace used to prepare a basement area into a livable, quiet space where she felt comfortable. Francisca was a quiet, gentle help in the nursery, always completing the most tedious of tasks, all the while showing the fruits of the Spirit—love, joy, peace, patience, kindness, goodness, faithfulness, gentleness, and self-control.

Francisca was well over eighty when she began to collapse. We knew that she needed to be in a place where she would receive physical help. Wallace helped contact her relatives still living in the Netherlands. As a Dutch victim of the Japanese invasion during World War II, Francisca could claim a retirement pension and medical care through the Dutch Act for War Victims.

We helped her pack her three suitcases, and Wallace took her to the airport. With no self-acclamation, she left with only quiet confidence and gladness for the life she led. Surely, Francisca was an example of Micah 6:8: "Do justly, love mercy, and walk humbly with your God."

God's Promise

God hath not promised skies always blue,
Flower strewn pathways all our lives through;
God hath not promised sun without rain,
Joy without sorrow, peace without pain.
But God hath promised strength for the day,
Rest for the labor, light for the way,
Grace for the trials, help from above,
Unfailing sympathy, undying love.

Annie J. Flint

ALL THE WAY,
MY SAVIOR LEADS ME

Socorro's desire was also to walk humbly with God. I cannot remember how Socorro found us high in the mountains of Haiti. She was tall, with beautiful black hair, soft olive skin and spoke with a slight accent—and spoke a lot! We knew her story was true; no one could create a story like the one she told us!

Socorro lived in Texas with her Mexican mother and several siblings. She attended a local university and when a group of excited, enthusiastic, convincing young people came professing to be "Children of God," she was touched. With great sincerity of heart she, along with others in her dormitory, gave or threw away all of their possessions and joined the Children of God to do God's will.

In the '60s there were many questionable cults following spectacular "divine revelations." These groups attracted the vulnerable, like Socorro, who were searching for something more and saw the institutional church as self-serving, existing largely for the sake of existing.

Socorro and a group of other students were put into a closed van with members of the sect who began giving directions about obeying the leaders and living apart from the evils of society—

untouched by the sins of the world. They were given cards from which to memorize scripture as well as rules and directives of the organization which would help them become "useful" Children of God. As questions were not permitted, the group did not know where they were going.

Several hours later, they arrived in a wide, uninhabited area where they found other members of the sect seeking God's will through isolation. After some days Socorro began to question her wisdom in leaving school just weeks before graduation to follow strangers whose teaching and conduct she found unreliable. She dared not express her discontent and soon realized she was a prisoner. She was assigned a "trainer" who followed her on walks around the field where she sometimes encountered neighboring farmers. She was encouraged to give her Christian witness to anyone she encountered. Here Socorro saw an opportunity.

She wrote a note explaining that she was being involuntarily held and needed help and slipped it in with her Bible verse cards. When she next went for a walk, she walked several paces in front of her trainer with her head down, reviewing her note cards. She headed towards the old farmer in his field, showing him one of her scripture verses, which was actually the note she had written. Socorro and her trainer then walked away.

Two days later Socorro made a break for it and ran the distance to the neighboring farmhouse. Fortunately, the old folks understood her, hiding her in their bathroom, and assured her they would not give her up to the sect. When the Children of God eventually came looking for Socorro, the farmers denied that she was there. The next day about twenty-five of the Children of God began a Jericho march around the farmhouse—praying, chanting, declaring, exhorting—asking God to deliver Socorro from doubt and evil.

Three days later, the farmers gave her bus fare and arranged for Socorro to get a pick-up truck ride into the nearest town. She took the bus home to her family.

It was our privilege to have Socorro stay for several months at the Mission while she stabilized emotionally and spiritually. God used her loving, obedient personality to care for the physical and spiritual needs of those in Haiti. We heard from her when she went back to Texas that she had married and had a fruitful ministry in the Mexican community there. She came back to Haiti and told us more stories of how "all the way, my Savior leads me…"

Do The Next Thynge

From an old English parsonage, Down by the sea,
There came in the twilight, message to me;
Its quaint Saxon legend, Deeply engraven,
Hath, as it seems to me, teaching from Heaven.
And on through the hours, The quiet words ring
Like a low inspiration-DO THE NEXT THYNGE

Many a questioning, many a fear,
Many a doubt, hath its quieting here.
Moment by moment, Let down from Heaven,
Time, opportunity, Guidance, are given.
Fear not tomorrows, Child of the King,
Trust them with Jesus, DO THE NEXT THYNGE

Do it immediately; Do it with prayer;
Do it reliantly, casting all care;
Do it with reverence, Tracing His Hand,
Who placed it before thee with Earnest command.
Stayed on Omnipotence, Safe 'neath His wing,
Leave all resultings, DO THE NEXT THYNGE

Looking to Jesus, ever serener,
(Working or suffering) Be thy demeanor,
In His dear presence, The rest of His calm,
The light of His countenance, Be thy psalm,
Strong in His faithfulness, Praise and sing,
Then, as He beckons thee, DO THE NEXT THYNGE

Authorn Unkown

ZEAL AND DETERMINATION

God must have a sense of humor. When He sent those who passed by, as I've said before, some could see their purpose immediately, others it took longer, and for a select few, well, they just seemed crazy. But to those who first met him, didn't John the Baptist seem crazy? He lived in the desert wearing camel's hair and eating locusts and wild honey (Mathew 3:4), yet he trusted the Father and proceeded with purpose. Alex seemed unstable, but we were sure that he, too, followed the Father.

Alex came to the Mission asking for a place to stay. He gave his Christian testimony, and as we got acquainted, we saw his effervescent personality. After supper, he told us about his family. They were descended from one of the great tobacco families in North Carolina and his family was still among the elite. Alex didn't really fit in with them since he had a heart for the poor and would invite the homeless to his home to have a shower and a bed. This caused embarrassment to his family, especially his grandmother. His uncles, who were doctors, saw his behavior as erratic and insisted he undergo brain surgery. Alex refused and enlisted in the Unites States Army. One of his favorite activities was to go around the base picking paper up off the ground, even the tiniest pieces. This behavior earned him a medical discharge.

However, Alex's efforts must have been missed because the Army ended up hiring someone to keep the base as clean as Alex did!

Alex showed us notes and dates written in his Bible when he had been imprisoned for preaching the Gospel. Once he was held in solitary in a small cell. Alex knew he needed exercise, so he took the tiny piece of soap in his washbowl, rubbed it on the floorboards, and slid back and forth, pretending he was skating. I still remember how Alex stood in our kitchen at the Mission, demonstrating how he skated in his cell. At one point he said, "I have been imprisoned eight times for preaching, and Paul only seven times—so you see, my record is better than St. Paul's!"

By midnight, Wallace and I were beginning to wonder if our guest was mentally stable or not. After showing Alex to his room and settling down for the night, I took the kerosene lamp to the kitchen and gathered up the butcher and carving knives and took them to our bedroom. Wallace was already sleeping, but I woke him to help me pull a chest in front of our door as I told my husband I was sure our guest was out of his mind.

Nothing happened that night, and Alex ended up staying with us several days. Before he left, he gave us a check for $500. He told us he was a pilot and expected to return from time-to-time to help the people of Haiti.

That time turned out to be at 2 a.m. a few months later. We awoke suddenly to the sound of loud calling and pounding on our door, "Pastor Turnbull! T-u-r-n-b-u-l-l!"

We rushed to the door, expecting an emergency, but there was Alex with a friend. He had put his watch on upside down, and thinking it was 6 a.m. instead of 12 a.m., had urged his friend to get dressed so they could go see the sunrise in the mountains.

Alex and his friend spent the day with us. He pulled Wallace aside and asked if Wallace could change a check for him? He admitted that he had run out of cash and explained that he was an ordained minister, and, since we both tithed, we could give a tenth of the $1000 check to him, and he was scripturally qualified to receive it. He asked to use a typewriter, and with an outdated machine and a faded, worn ribbon he wrote: THIS IS A CHECK. PAY TO THE ORDER OF WALLACE TURNBULL THE SUM OF $1000. SIGNED, ALEX…

Wallace gave Alex the $100 tithe from the donation and forwarded the check to the mission office in the US for receipting. The bank, who knew us, honored it. God's promise to supply all of your needs is sometimes kept through the strangest circumstances.

Whenever Alex arrived, we came to expect excitement. He was a very lovable, interesting, and generous friend, but was always full of surprises. Once he brought an ex-Army friend with him who was a slow giant of a man and claimed he had power given to him by God. Alex went with his friend to a funeral of a young child in Port-au-Prince. They walked to the front of the packed church, bent over the open casket of the dead child and began to pray for his resurrection! Alex told us later that even he thought such action was unscriptural.

After Jesus, Alex was passionate about flying and his two Collie dogs. However, his sometimes reckless behavior put them both in jeopardy. He lost his Florida driver's license after racing the police with the two huge dogs on the hood of his car. Then he lost his U.S. pilot's license by buzzing Daytona Beach. The loss of his licenses didn't stop Alex from traveling, however.

Once Alex lost his pilot's license, he would charter a plane from Miami to Haiti and then, once in the air, he would demand that the pilot let him fly the plane. On one of these chartered flights, he stopped on an island to refuel. Impetuously following his free spirit, Alex went down to the beach. He took off his clothes, and wearing only a strategically-placed conch shell, stretched out in the sand. The sounds of the sea slapping on the shore, the cloudless blue sky, and the warm sand quickly put Alex into a sound sleep for four hours. The pilot, irritated, had just let him sleep because he couldn't leave without fuel—which Alex had to pay for—and the pilot wouldn't be paid until he completed the chartered flight. When Alex woke up, he was terribly burned. He spent the night on the island suffering from a high fever. The next day when he arrived in Florida, he admitted himself to the Veteran's Hospital. Alex went into the hospital to have his burns treated, but his medical records show he was eventually moved to the 6th floor for the mentally unstable. It took two weeks for Alex's burns to heal and then another two weeks for him to be released. Eventually, he made it back to the Mission and made a generous donation.

Alex chuckled over coffee as he explained how he had made the money. "The people at the hospital thought I was crazy!" he exclaimed. "But while I was there, I sold my Coco-Cola stock and made $20,000! It was all God's will." I remember how Alex's donations often came in answer to prayer and helped complete several projects.

Alex's other love was his Collies. Everyone enjoyed the remarkable performances of the dogs who were delighted to climb the ladder and go down the slide. Alex went everywhere with them. During one year's Fourth of July celebration I heard dogs barking and then heard Alex's very loud voice calling, "Praise God! The Baptists are having a party!" We had no idea Alex was anywhere in Haiti, but we were happy to see him.

On another one of Alex's visits to Haiti, he had piloted his chartered flight into Port-au-Prince, the airport guards asked for identification, landing authorization, and other papers, and he was exceedingly impudent. They told him he was under arrest and must go with them to the police headquarters. Forgetting his dogs, Alex and the pilot started to run, jumped in a cab, and raced to the Cedars of Lebanon restaurant. Alex knew the hostess and rushed through the restaurant to hide in the kitchen. A police car full of military men pulled up and began searching the restaurant, interrupting the hostess who was serving of her famous kebabs and threatening to get rough with her if she didn't turn Alex over to them. Sisi bristled at the threat, grabbed a large bottle of wine from the shelf, and broke it over the policeman's head while Alex and the pilot slipped out the back door. They took a cab to the Mission on the Kenscoff Road.

Now, when they arrived, we, of course, knew nothing of what had transpired, so we welcomed him as usual and showed him to the guest room, which has an adjoining toilet and shower. Accustomed to Alex's strange behaviors, we still wondered why he said he wanted to take a bath. The great scarcity of water at the Mission was a constant problem, and we cringed as we heard the water running behind the bathroom's locked door. We continued to wonder why Alex was taking an hour-long bath until a police car arrived with four military officers asking for the man who ran away from the airport!

Wallace explained Alex's eccentric behavior and his need for medication to the police. Alex never came out, but because the military knew they could trust us, they said they would leave him in our charge for the night, but we were responsible to have him at the airport before 10 a.m. the next day.

The next morning, Alex roared with laughter as he told us about running away from the Haitian police, but he was also distraught as he remembered his dogs had been left on the plane overnight.

When we arrived at the airport, the first thing Alex wanted to do was find his dogs. Both of the Collies were fine and happy to see him. We, including the dogs, went into the office and waited. When the police chief entered the room, he was followed by six armed guards who crowded into the small office. The chief declared that Alex must file a flight plan to leave Haiti immediately. I was acting as interpreter and related the command to Alex.

Alex told me that the police had no right to make him leave and that I was to tell the police chief that he was not going, which I hesitatingly did.

The police chief told me that he understood Alex was mentally unstable and was not responsible for his actions; he did not want to arrest him and take him to prison, but if Alex did not leave, he would have no choice.

The scene became tense and threatening as Alex insisted that he would not leave. I translated Alex's words to the determined, angry guards, "I will give my collies an attack command, and they will leap at the guard's throats in a manner they have never imagined." Knowing the fear many Haitians have for dogs, and recognizing their resentment and annoyance of having the dogs in their office, I feared the worst as I translated Alex's threat.

Immediately, four of the officers drew and cocked their guns saying in Creole, "Let's shoot the dogs and tie up the man." At those words, all the staff in the office fled the scene. I stepped into a partially-protected corner, translating, "Alex, they are going to kill your dogs. Please, they are serious about shooting! Please agree to leave." The dogs were more important to Alex than his own life or the lives of those who were there. Alex hesitated, shocked and frightened. The guards were still ready to shoot, and I kept yelling, "If you don't agree, they *will* kill the dogs!"

I felt a great relief when Alex finally said, "Don't shoot my dogs. I'll do whatever is necessary."

I insisted that Alex let the pilot do the exit formalities. Even so, notes were made and formalized that Alex should never return to Haiti. As I walked with Alex and his dogs to the plane, Alex whispered in my ear as he hugged me, "I will be back."

We did not hear from Alex until there was a government change in Haiti; suddenly he was on the telephone asking if we thought it was safe for him to come back! He wanted to avoid the Haitian airports so had bought a seaplane. He wanted to commute from the U.S. to Haiti so he could establish a Christian school, and he hoped we could help him persuade the Haitian military to let him land on water near a small coastal village. We explained that such was not done in Haiti and it would not be possible. Alex was determined, however, and since he was on the run from his family, he soon appeared on our doorstep at the Mission.

The Mission had a very good rapport with Colonel Danache, the head of Haiti's Air Force, who controlled all air travel in Haiti. I did not want to put that relationship in jeopardy as a result of Alex's erratic behavior. With Alex listening, I called Colonel Danache's office and asked if I might bring to see him an American who needed authorization. The Colonel said he had later engagements, but he could meet with us that morning, if we came quickly. The call ended, and I excused myself to another room, where I could secretly call the Colonel again.

I was shaking with anxiety, hoping the phone call would go through, that the Colonel would answer, and that we would have a good line connection. By a miracle, the Colonel did answer. "Colonel, I am coming, but I cannot recommend the man with me as mentally reliable and competent." "I understand, Madame." And the call ended.

When we arrived at the military headquarters, Alex brought both Collies with him on leashes. A guard told us we could not take the dogs inside. Without hesitation, Alex handed the leashes to the guard and said to me, "Tell the guard he must keep the dogs for us." I did, and the guard responded, "Absolutely not." Another soldier nearby caught my eye, and I pleaded the case of the "naive foreigner who needed help." He gave us permission to tie the dogs nearby.

Inside, Colonel Danache offered all the graciousness for which Haitian officials are renowned. After introductions, Alex requested permission to the Miragoane coast as a seaplane landing zone where he could fly in and out of Haiti. The colonel asked, "May I see your pilot's license?" There was none. Embarrassed, Alex fumbled in his pockets and unleashed a row of cards, permits, and credentials about ten feet long. As it unwound and fell to the floor, Colonel Danache laughed, offered his congratulations, and assured Alex that as soon as he could present a valid pilot's license, he would be glad to take an application for his request. The Haitian officials are masters in such situations. I thanked Colonel Danache and told Alex, "The door is not closed, but you have some homework to do."

That was the last time we saw Alex. We have missed his positive, happy assurance and wished that others might have more of Alex's zeal and determination.

Someone cried, "Where must the seed be sown to bring the most fruit when it is grown?"

The Master heard as He said and smiled, "Go plant it for Me in the heart of a child."

Unknown

MELON FOR LUNCH

Only God could pull so many details together for the furthering of His kingdom. What continues to amaze me is how He cares about fulfilling the desires of our hearts in the process.

Standing near the door of the Mountain Maid Self Help Outlet, a man with a Dutch accent asked to no one in particular, "Do you speak English?"

My son Wally was walking through the outlet at the time. He paused and took in the man's appearance: He wore tan khaki clothes, his shoes were untied, and his khaki cap was pulled low over his eyes, but there was a glint of joy in his eyes.

"Yes, I speak English," Wally answered. "Can I help you?"

"Yes, perhaps you can. I am Aart Van Wingerden, and I have a Christian organization called Double Harvest. I was referred to the Mission because I understand we share an interest in agriculture."

The stranger's name caught Wally's attention. "Van Wingerden? From North Carolina? Known for your greenhouses?"

"That's me!"

There was an instant friendship and bond between Wally and Aart. Wally knew his wife, Betty, was in town shopping for groceries, but such immediate bonding knit with deep Christian understanding demanded that Wally invite Aart to lunch at his house. However, when Wally got to the kitchen, the cupboards were totally bare. Whoops! But with the wonderful conversation and newfound friendship, the lunch of melon and coffee became a feast.

I remember my first conversation with Aart. After he had mentioned that his sons would be interested in working in Haiti, I asked about his family.

With his Dutch accent, he said, "My vife is Cora. Ve haf sixteen children, twelve boys en four girls." Thinking that surely it was combined families—his, hers, ours—or that he may be including grandchildren, I asked, "Did you—?" But before I could finish, Aart proudly answered, "Ve made dem von by von."

He soon told us that after emigrating from Holland to the United States after World War II, he had begun with little English and very few resources. He knew Christ as Savior and became active in a small church. He was soon teaching a Sunday school class but felt that through the lessons he was learning to obey God and be true to the Scriptures. One Sunday, he arrived home from church and said, "Vife, Cora, ve do not love vell!" 1 John 3:16-17 cried out in his soul. "By this, we know love, because He laid down His life for us. And we also ought to lay down our lives for the brethren. But whoever has this world's goods, and sees his brother in need, and shuts up his heart from him, how does the love of God abide in him?"

In response to God's call, Aart and Cora packed up the children (perhaps less than half the total had been born), left a prosperous greenhouse flower business in California, and moved to Indonesia to help the poor. From Indonesia, the ever-growing family moved to Honduras, and then back to the United States. Once the older children married and were ready to take over some of Aart's greenhouses, he established Double Harvest. The intent was for him and his sons to use profits from the greenhouses in the United States, and to invest them in agricultural projects in Third World communities to increase food production and help grow the local economies.

When Aart learned that Haiti was the poorest country in the Western world and that World Health charts listed Haiti at the very bottom for protein consumption, and second from the bottom for caloric intake per capita, he decided to visit. Aart loved children and was appalled to learn that two out of every ten children born in Haiti died before age five. He had become a highly successful businessman because he carefully studied all the information related to his goals before investing. When he learned through his studies that eighty percent of Haiti's children's illness and death was caused by malnutrition he immediately said, "Ve teach Haiti to grow more food!" Aart was sure he could teach the Haitians how to produce more corn, millet, and beans.

From his family to farming, Aart did everything big. He believed that only big farming and big production would improve Haiti's food situation. Wally insisted that "small is beautiful." The "little man," the peasant farmer, who was farming on an eroded hillside with no capital for investment, needed to grow cash crops to provide essentials for his family. This became a friendly debate between the two men who formed a partnership that day over a lunch of only melon.

It was clear that Aart had been sent to the Mission on the Kenscoff Road. Only God, Maker of Heaven and Earth, could have orchestrated such a meeting. Over the years, it was incredible to see how these two men complimented one another, and of course, the Haitian people benefited greatly from their successes. Aart invited Wally to go to the United States and see the Van Wingerden Greenhouses. It was amazing to see acres of poinsettias and other flowers ready for delivery to big box stores, grocery stores, and other markets across the United States.

Wally worked with Aart to evaluate the flower-growing possibilities of Haiti. Finding that florists in Haiti were buying more than a million dollars per year of flowers from Colombia. Aart agreed to give technical and material aid for a pilot project. The mountain climate of Haiti was agreeable for growing chrysanthemums, so the Mission once again created a Self Help Project that would help families have an income to buy food to feed their families. While the Mission produced scores of plants from stock imported from Aart's greenhouses, local farmers were taught how to prepare even, small plots on their steep mountainside land. Water had to be carried in five-gallon cans from distant springs, but farmers soon learned their efforts paid off. The flowers grew well and the income selling them allowed farmers to feed their families. After experimentation, demonstration, and participation, the florists of Haiti no longer bought imported chrysanthemums grown in Colombia!

Aart had also established a large farm in the lowlands of Haiti. He brought John Deere equipment from the United States and crew to maintain them. There he grew corn, millet, and beans in quantities far beyond anything ever known in Haiti. Aart also grew tomatoes. The tomato-growing part of the project was so successful that some businessmen invested with capital to become subcontractors. Many Haitian recipes traditionally call for tomato paste, so they became the suppliers for a factory making tomato paste and ketchup. Even when the plant faltered and later closed, there was still a demand for tomatoes, so open-bed truckloads of tomatoes were then transported across the Dominican Republic border to the factory in Santo Domingo.

I'm not sure if Aart ever admitted that "small is beautiful." He came to see that "you can't eat a tree" was flawed logic when he says how erosion causes hunger. He began growing tropical tree seedlings for the lowlands, thus supplementing the efforts of the Mission on the Kenscoff Road and becoming the leading tree provider for the whole country. Both men saw success using his preferred methodology, the children of Haiti were fed, and Aart and Wally were fast friends.

The last time we saw Aart was at his home in Asheville, NC where he was designing plans for advanced irrigation. His concern for hungry children in Haiti continued, but so like the Aart we had always known and loved, he did not dwell on the problem but showed us his plan for his next solution.

The Van Wingerden children are now grandparents with children and grandchildren of their own reared to work, to be creative, and to remember the needy children of the world. Cora raised the first sixteen, but her legacy will continue. She could show you a picture and tell you the name and birthday of each of her 143 grandchildren! Because of this couple who passed by the Mission, many other children have not only been taught how to walk but more importantly, where to walk. They have been shown love and are thus better able to understand how to give of themselves and to love others for "God so loved the world that He gave His only Son" (John 3:16), which continues to be the message of the Mission.

The Inner Side

The inner side of every cloud
Is bright and shining.
I therefore turn my clouds about,
And always wear them inside out
To show the lining.

Ellen Thorneycroft Fowler Felton

UNLIKELY EATS

The first time I saw Euell Gibbons was in a television commercial for Post Grape-Nuts cereal. He was standing in the snow picking nuts off a bush and talking about the wonders of eating from nature. I knew he had become an icon as a highly respected naturalist, that he, more than anyone else, got people thinking, talking, and eating wild foods. I had read some of his many magazine articles from *National Geographic, Organic Gardening and Farming, National Wildlife Magazine*, and others. We owned a copy of his first book *Stalking the Wild Asparagus*, giving information on how to find, gather, and prepare various wild foods.

The next time I saw Euell Gibbons was when he and his wife Freda came to stay some days at the Mission on the Kenscoff Road. Euell was happy to learn something of the Mission's involvement with a snail harvesting project. Those pesky, slimy little creatures had become a plague to the peasant mountain farmers. In season, they ate more of the farmers' crops than the rats that had always held first place, destroying twenty percent of crops in Haiti. The Petit Gris snail had been brought to Haiti in colonial days by the French escargots lovers who still feel that no restaurant is proper if it does not include escargots on the menu.

We explained to Euell how "one man's garbage is another man's feast" became real when Felix, a restaurant owner in New York City, came to Haiti looking for escargots. Felix winced while talking to Wally when he saw us gathering and squashing snails before they would destroy the flower beds we jealously regarded on the Mission grounds. Wally immediately realized that Felix was one of those who had been sent to the Mission. He instantly recognized in Felix a solution to the snail problem. However, there were still many obstacles to getting the snails relocated. Sure, Wally could get peasants to gather the snails, but then what? Closing them in tin or glass would be expensive for shipping, and many of the snails would die. To be proper escargots, the snail had to be cleaned and purged before it could be eaten. All that could be worked out, but how to contain those slow but insistent little movers? The saying is true: "As slow and determined as a snail." We had to find some way to contain those creatures and make them stop escaping.

Having lived with snails in Haiti, Wally was aware that during the dry season the snail sealed itself inside its shell and became dormant until there was moisture. Ah-hah! The answer was to make the snails go dormant by putting them in cages with fans blowing dry air on them. It worked! Wally called in local basket makers who helped him design the right-sized basket with a tight lid. The basket weavers were delighted to find a job. And as far as gathering the snails—the local population could not believe that anyone would give them money for snails. First, the farmers came with five-gallon cans of snails. It was when they began to come with gunny sacks full that Wally decided on a fair system with rules. Widows and the most destitute had first chance. Felix's business became wholesale, and people were hired and trained to weigh the snails, ensure their quality, maintain their cages, pack, and ship many tons of snails a year to the Big Apple.

Can you imagine the excitement and wonder this project brought to the people of the mountains? I smile as I remember hearing one old woman unloading a heavy gunny sack of snails, those treacherous garden pests, off her donkey, explaining to an on-looker, "Oh *wi*, it is what the rich people in New York eat."

The simple mountain people had never heard of Euell Gibbons—they had never read his books and were not members of his Wild Food Association, but they did know that snails ate too much of their crops. They knew that by sending the snails to the "rich people in New York," they could buy some beans and oil to put with their cornmeal mush or buy the essentials to send their children to school.

While at the Mission on the Kenscoff Road, Euell Gibbons followed his usual technique to research wild foods—ask local people and exchange information. As usual, he and his wife Freda would experiment and invent new ways to use pigweed, benzolive leaves and pods, wild yams, and other plants used by the indigenous people. I think that even Euell Gibbons was startled to learn that cats were much relished in rural villages. As missionaries entertained by local "notables" we had often been served cat meat and had repeatedly felt violated when our own cats were stolen for the stew pot.

Being a well-informed, ardent naturalist himself, Wallace was also a convinced creationist. Neither Euell Gibbons nor Wallace was a great talker, but Wallace could not miss the opportunity to ask the world-renowned naturalist his question. "Euell, what do you find in nature as the greatest proof of intelligent design?" Without hesitation, Euell answered, "In all my long life of research, I have never, never, found any living organism that does not have a symbiotic relationship with another." With such agreement, the two men went on to speak of the wonder of God's perfect ecology, His comprehensive creation, and God's perfect plan for mankind.

Dead To Self

If I would bear both gain and loss,
In freedom from both bitterness and pride,
Then there must be no shrinking from the cross,
And I must by Thy side, dear Lord, abide.

From sinful self I must, indeed, be free,
and kind, to serve, and Thy full glory see.
Naught in myself is good, indeed, I find.
Oh, reign within my heart, Thou Christ Divine.

I ask not, Lord, for easy paths to tread.
I ask Thee for a willing heart, instead,
To do Thy will, whatever it may be,
Discerning clearly Thy best plan for me
or what Thy will may be.

Margaret McKenzie

MADAME MARGUERITE

Madame Marguerite was a refreshing delight each time she passed by the Mission on the Kenscoff Road. With her amusing don't-miss-that-I-am-French accent she seemed always to have a wonderful story to tell. Madame had traveled with her American husband, Scott, to many parts of the world—in Haiti, he was the director of the USAID. All Madame needed was an ear to listen and an occasional question to lead her on! With all the gestures and demonstrative voice of a French Madame, she could be misunderstood as unfeeling and shallow. Like when she exclaimed that she'd never been in a place like this (Haiti)! "There is sooo much dust and dirt! Even Asa, my Indonesian cook, refuses to go to the market for supplies! Now he is a courageous man—always travels with us, but this is the first place he finds it too dirty!"

Or when she'd tell you that her six servants were also dirty and needed soap. "I do my best to get them to be clean. At first, I was surprised that after I gave each one a bar of soap some were asking me for another bar of soap the next day! So—I could see perhaps they were selling it, sending it to their family, or giving it to a girlfriend? Now, every morning I ask them to line up and hold the bar of soap in an outstretched hand so I can see they have it and that they are using it!"

But when asked why she and her husband had six servants in addition to her chef who traveled with her, she'd say, "They need employment. They have families and children." She delighted in telling the story of the new baby. "You know, when one came and told me his wife had a new baby, I gave him $50 to help. I knew he could use it. But, three months later, when he again told me his wife had a new baby, I chided him for having 'too many wives' but gave him $50 to help out. Now can you imagine almost every month one of the servants comes to say that his wife had a new baby? So with the over-population in Haiti, I decided to use the money and give them contraceptives! Now, tell me, do you think that is wrong? I was raised Catholic, so maybe I need to pray for forgiveness."

One of our more serious conversations followed, as Wallace and I told her the reason we need a Savior is because each of us needs forgiveness. I hope she came to understand that our offense to God is not the kind of help we give to the poor, but if we do not accept and obey His revelation in the Flesh—Jesus.

Madame's visits always began with a detailed account of Jako, her parrot who ruled her life. He asked for crackers, but refused all kinds, "all except those cute little yellow ones that look like goldfish! Oh yes, he is spoiled, but you know I love him, so I have to buy those expensive imported goldfish ones! Oh *oui*, he is like me; he wants the best!"

In spite of her flighty mannerisms, we found Madame to be a person able to identify good values. She also enjoyed needling those who took themselves too seriously. One afternoon while spending some time with an international representative living for a few weeks at the Hotel Villa Creole, her husband Scott chose to enjoy the pool while the ladies visited in the shade. When he finished, he again used the friend's room to dress and go out to join Madame and her friend. "Let me tell you what happened! The very next day, 'So and So,' who thinks she is such an elite, phoned to declare her embarrassment in telling me something very bad." The woman thought it was her duty to tell Madame how her husband Scott was seen coming out of the bedroom of a certain woman at the hotel!

"Now can you imagine, the woman who phoned me was supposed to be my friend—oh *oui*. But do you know what I told her? I told her '*Merci beaucoup*—I do hope that she was young and beautiful—it will be good for Scott, and he is so deserving!' That is exactly what I told her so now she is *not* my friend because she wanted to be a troublemaker!"

During her time in Haiti, Madame became an avid supporter of the "Mountain Maids" and their fine hand-made embroidered tablecloths. She loved the handwork and couldn't resist when she found a new color or new design. Perhaps she loved them so because she, too, was a gifted embroiderer and knew the labor involved in making something beautiful. She bought dozens of tablecloths while in Haiti and sent many others to come and shop.

Madame might not have known the embroidery ladies by name, but she knew them by their work. She could tell that these were made by this one and those by another and still others by someone else. She could tell that a particular lady was having trouble with the hem-stitching and all while exclaiming how abominable it was, she would sit with the lady and teach her to do it well.

Once when visiting her in her home, I asked if she enjoyed using her lovely tablecloths. "Use them! *Non, non*! Not possible. They would be ruined." She opened a closet to show shelves and shelves of the lovely colored cloths neatly put away, each wrapped in its own plastic bag.

We are guarded on all sides by His presence
For He is:
BEFORE us (Isaiah 48:17)
BEHIND us (Isaiah 30:21)
To the RIGHT of us (Psalm 16:8)
To the LEFT of us (Job 23:9)
ABOVE us (Psalm 36:7)
UNDERNEATH us (Deuteronomy 33:27)
and in this dispensation, even
WITHIN us (I Corinthians 3:16)
I thank Him for it.

Ebba Riese

GO AWAY PIGGY

D o you remember how the Haitian pig was used as the toilet? Our dear friend, Dr. David found this out the hard way.

He had become a close friend and advisor and passed by the Mission to be part of our expansion. The depths of his insight and the breadth of his vocabulary were equaled only by his voice! His formal dress—always a coat and bow tie—were in keeping with his stance of authority. I remember when once speaking of a situation I said, "I am glad I was not there, I might have spit!" His deep voice replied with authority, "My sister, it would have been holy spit…"

In the most primitive of circumstances, we appreciated the support of Dr. David and his group of five friends who came as advisors. To Dr. David supper was always dinner—even in the kitchen on a tin-topped table with plastic plates, and it still demanded coat, white shirt, and a bow tie.

Dr. David was a man of deep spiritual insight and vision, which sometimes got buried beneath the superfluous academic over-kill. I remember a time we were discussing a strategy to create ten mission schools for approximately 1000 children. David came to the meeting with a plan for both a national and international educational program to change national statistics, which included not only primary and secondary schools, but vocational and university education as well. We sighed, and we wished he could advise us on a basic literacy program for the Mission on a non-existent budget.

Now remembering, I look back and think that Dr. David was to us, to Haiti, like Elijah must have been to the children of Israel as he proclaimed his news in his burly way. With Dr. David, God brought us along so that the program and we might grow together.

On a trip by Jeep to visit some of Haiti's most isolated and difficult areas, Wallace and other visiting advisors tried to give Dr. David preference. Days in the Willys Jeep with no seat springs and no air conditioning on roads that little more than rocky dust trails strained Dr. David's dignity.

In areas where pigs foraging in desert-like areas were the only means of sanitation, Wallace warned the men to take rocks with them when they "went aside to the bushes" to throw at the pigs. Waiting, hungry pigs were often unwilling to wait for the man to leave before getting the pig's share of the waste. More than once, men had suffered as the waiting pig grabbed whatever might "hang down!" The friends waited nearby when they saw Dr. David start toward the bushes. They saw him first take off his trousers and hang them on some bushes, followed by his underwear. Then they heard a couple of pigs grunt as they anxiously followed him! They heard him say "Go away piggy, go away." Later, "Piggy, no! No! Go away!" Almost crying, "Piggy, go! Go away!" and then with his great voice of authority he demanded, "No, pig! Go!"

We are so thankful to all of those who, like Dr. David, left the familiar to step into the unknown of Haiti, for as Philippians 2:13 says, "for it is God who works in you, both to will and to work for His good pleasure."

My Kitchen Prayer

Man shall not live by bread alone
Our Lord and Master said,
But by the living Word of God,
Our souls must needs be fed.

So as I cook and serve the meals,
I will sincerely pray.
That I shall give, along with food,
Some Christ-like love today.

Now as I clear the meal away,
And wash the pots and pans,
Dear God, please cleanse my thoughts and
Heart with thine own loving hands.

Man shall not live by bread alone,
So we do pray, dear Lord,
"Please make us very hungry
For a knowledge of thy Word."

Nellie Pease Gorbett

FRIENDSHIP ROAD

Elias was a commanding personage who found his way to Haiti through many countries, many languages, and many experiences. The first eighteen years of his life were spent in Palestine.

Born in a well-to-do Arab family, Elias had the best education in Ramallah, Palestine. Because the Greek Orthodox priesthood usually followed family lines, it was expected that young Elias would follow his two Greek Orthodox uncles as a priest. Even as his handsome beard matched his graying hair, he told us of his happy childhood. He told us that his private nursemaid was an Orthodox nun who took him to church every day, and sometimes all day! He was aware that priests' families lived more "as the rich" without much involvement with the poor. Somehow through his mother, he had come to be aware and kindly concerned about the poor people of his surroundings. When he became eighteen, he inwardly fought between pleasing his family and following the "elite priesthood" or following the less-conventional side of his Orthodox faith and serving the poor.

The decision was answered for him one day when a family member came by his home and demanded that the entire family leave in his car. Israel was taking over Ramallah, and the family had to leave immediately, or they feared they would never get out. Without time to prepare, the family was packed into the car, and they left. Elias showed us a picture of their fine family home that had been taken over as Israeli police quarters.

Elias was still at an early age when he was sponsored by an American Quaker and taken as a refugee to Pendleton Hill in Pennsylvania where he lived and worked for some years. He eventually married a young woman from Arkansas who was also working there.

Elias' superior early education and the administrative skills learned at Pendleton knit together with his concern for the poor and qualified him to work with international aid agencies.

When Elias and his family came to the Mission on the Kenscoff Road, he came from Pakistan, Africa, Latin America, and Washington, DC. Elias knew people of influence in every country. He brought with him global acquaintances and the riches of a good name—uprightness, experience, wisdom, and personal sacrifice. Elias and Mary Ellen, his wife, were good examples of the scriptural admonition, "A good name is to be chosen rather than great riches."

It soon became clear that Elias and Mary Ellen were among those who passed by the Mission on the Kenscoff Road, those who had been sent. Mary Ellen took advantage of living close to the Haitian mountain people to finish her research for her PhD in sociology. Their son Steve had spent time in Jerusalem and Cairo and took a university post as a professor of Arab Affairs. Their daughter, Melisa, completed her nursing and continued in HIV research at the National Institute of Health in DC until her triplets were born.

Elias spoke both French and Creole, so with his experience and administrative skills, he was able to step in and help with the wide-spread Food for Work projects following the example of the Mission. One project was working on a new road to Jacmel.

The road was later enlarged and asphalted by France and become known as *Route de l'Amitie* (Friendship Road). It spanned twenty-five miles over steep, mountainous terrain. Elias was able to help thousands of families by using alternating schedules to keep hundreds of local people working at a time, armed with picks, shovels, truck axle bars, and wheelbarrows to dig and haul away boulders from the mountainside. Elias was careful to make sure that fifty percent of the workers were women. Except for the extreme digging, the women accomplished more than the men. They carried heavy loads, very large stones, and tons of earth on their heads. The mountain people industriously followed Elias' direction and motivation. Some of the secondary roads took extra work. So Elias gave heavy hammers to some of the older people who would sit all day breaking stones into gravel to put on the steep dirt parts of the road.

The Mission encouraged Elias to extend the project to erosion control. He supplied tons of *Pois Congo*, Congo bean, seed and a few thousand tropical oak tree seedlings which the people planted on the steep roadside banks. With Elias' help, the Mission was able to keep families of other areas from starving since it was during the years of famine. The people always seem to live on the edge in Haiti, working hard to simply survive. For many of them, existence is something to eat and a bit of water for today. They understand the depth of the prayer: "Give us this day our daily bread."

Elias is no longer in Haiti, but the benefits of what he did remain. The people of the mountains, as well as we at the Mission, knew that Elias was surely one of those who had been sent to the Mission on the Kenscoff Road.

Being A Missionary

Out where the loneliness presses round me,
Looking on sights that are sordid and drear-
Strangely abiding...yet, surely God called me.
Why do I wonder if Jesus is near?

Strangeness of living...Strangeness of people...
Have I not come with a Gospel cheer?
Why is my heart then depressed with it burden?
Isn't my Comrade...My Jesus...out here?

God, teach me quickly to do without friendship;
How to let go of those things that are dear;
How to be rid of this self that so binds me;
Surely, my Master...My Jesus...is here.

He, Who is God, took the form of a servant,
Humbled Himself unto death, with fear;
Lonely, forsaken, despised, and rejected...
My blessed Saviour...My Jesus...came here.

Father, forgive me my failure in serving;
Heartache, depression, regrets all disappear!
Born of the Cross, a new courage infills me.
Jesus...my Victory...my Life...IS here!

Moody Bible Institute Monthly

DHAHRAN CONNECTION

Through the years many college students came to the Mission seeking experience, truth, internships, and direction for their lives. We might never have remembered the pretty young blonde student who had returned to college in the United States if her parents hadn't contacted us from Saudi Arabia to say "thank you" for receiving their daughter who had written them about Haiti and the Mission on the Kenscoff Road.

The young student was from Dhahran, the only place in Saudi Arabia where a Christian church was permitted. Her parents lived on the Aramco oil compound and helped in the church. Scores of international Christians worshiped together there and they understood the great commission: "Go therefore and make disciples of all the nations, baptizing them in the name of the Father and of the Son and of the Holy Spirit, teaching them to observe all things that I have commanded you; and lo, I am with you always." After their daughter visited Haiti, they decided to support the Mission on the Kenscoff Road. We were reminded of the prophecy, "and a little child will lead them," as through the years they became a major sponsor of the Mission.

A few years later, Wallace was invited as the director of the Mission, to go to Saudi Arabia and be part of a missions conference for the English-speaking congregation. No women visitors were allowed, so he made the trip alone. It was quite a long process: traveling to Texas to the main Aramco office where he was given his visa, along with other precautionary "do's" and "don'ts" as he was reminded that his profession was now "educator" rather than "reverend" and the title was omitted from his name.

This trip was particularly interesting to Wallace because when he was a very young child in 1926-1927 he had lived in Palestine with his missionary parents. In 1926, his father had met with Faisal, Prince of Transjordan who gave him authorization to cross the Arabian Desert in an automobile with the help of a Bedouin guide. On the flight, Wallace had time to reflect on how his parents had a great burden for the people of Saudi Arabia. He had copies of letters and poetry prayers his mother had written expressing deep concern for the people of Arabia. Their work in Arabia had been cut short after his mother's sudden death, and the grieving family returned to the United States. But now, here he was, traveling back with the unique opportunity to visit and briefly minister in Arabia.

Following that visit, the church in Dhahran took Haiti as their missions project, praying and generously supporting the Mission's annual budget for the outreach ministry. All this because one faithful young woman was one who passed by, who had not come, but had surely been sent to the Mission on the Kenscoff Road.

The Regions Beyond

To the regions beyond I must go, I must go
Where the story has never been told;
To the millions that never have heard of His love,
I must tell the sweet story of old.

To the hardest of places He calls me to go,
Never thinking of comfort or ease;
The world may pronounce me a dreamer, a fool,
Enough if the Master I please.

Oh, you that are spending your leisure and powers
In those pleasures so foolish and fond;
Awake from your selfishness, folly and sin,
And go to the regions beyond.

There are other lost sheep that the Master must bring,
And to them must the message be told;
He sends me to gather them out of all lands,
And welcome them back to His fold.

To the regions beyond I must go, I must go,
Till the world, all the world,
His salvation shall know.

Albert B. Simpson

NAIM

Naim was a man with a clear gospel message, a caring heart, and a soulful passion for Arabs all over the world. We told him of the Arabs in Haiti. He recognized that the Arabs represented a sizable "unreached people group." He became concerned about the many Arab professionals, merchants, and business people settled and continually immigrating from Damascus and Bethlehem to Haiti. He was sure they needed to hear the gospel message of hope from an Arab. It was a long trip from Jerusalem to Port-au-Prince, Haiti, but one he had to take.

Anyone visiting Haiti soon found that many of the larger businesses in the capital city were owned and run by a tightly connected Middle Eastern population. Many of the Haitian Arabs married within their own community or sent to the "old country" for a spouse. Family and business seemed to be their life. Most were not Muslim and usually turned to the Roman Catholic church for marriage and funerals. Much of the money of Haiti was in the hands of the Arab population, which was a closely-knit society of extended family. Due to our long-time relationship, the Mission was able to introduce Naim to the "Godfather" of that important population.

With the Godfather's recommendation and introduction, Naim had an immediate, warm, Arab-style welcome. He shared the Arabic Bibles he had brought and made himself available for personal and group gatherings. They liked Naim, and gradually some began to share their disappointments, frustrations, and fears. Many were homesick; some found their family-arranged marriages incompatible, others were unable to adjust to living in a foreign land and felt resentful of the primitive culture around them. Gradually, they emptied their hearts and exposed their deep fear of the Haitian Vodou, which they found all around them. They confessed that they had never felt the need nor taken the time to reflect about Jehovah, the God of their ancestors. They also knew that Vodou worship of evil spirits, sorcerers, and curses was not right.

Naim could not stay, but the Truth, which he had planted, remained. He had heard their many questions, and he had answered them from the Scripture. Importantly, he had answered them in "the Arab way." Some of the Arab population of Haiti began to hear the invitation of the Savior: "Come unto Me..."

A few years later we were invited to Naim's ordination. We found ourselves in a fine, old monumental Lutheran church in the middle of the city of Jerusalem for the consecration of Naim as the Arab Archbishop of Jerusalem. The Creole proverb says *"Nan mitan diri, ti wòch goute grès"*—"in the rice, a pebble tastes the fat." It means something like "thanks to important friends, a poor man tastes the good life." We attended an impressive ceremony in a Jewish land because God had caused an Arab Christian to pass by the Mission on the Kenscoff Road.

ONE DAY AT A TIME!

One day at a time, with its failures and fears,
With its hurts and mistakes, with its weakness and tears,
With its portion of pain, and its burden of care;
One day at a time, we must meet and must bear.

One day at a time, to be patient and strong,
To be calm under trial, and sweet under wrong;
Then its toiling shall pass, and its sorrow shall cease;
It shall darken and die, and the night shall bring peace.

One day at a time—but the day is so long,
And the heart is not brave, and the soul is not strong,
O piteous Christ, be near all the way;
Give courage and patience, and strength for the day.

Swift comes His answer, so clear and so sweet;
"Yes, I'll be with you, your troubles to meet;
I will not forget you, nor fail you, nor grieve;
I will not forsake you; I never will leave."

Not yesterday's load, we are called on to bear,
Nor the morrow's uncertain and shadowy care;
Why should we look forward, or back with dismay?
Our needs, as our mercies, are but for the day.

One day at a time, and the day is His day;
He has numbered its hours, though they haste or delay.
His grace is sufficient, we walk not alone;
As the day, so the strength that He gives His own.

Annie Johnson Flint

THE STRANGER,
THE ANGEL

Do you remember my story of Gary and Gail who had their wedding rings made in Haiti? When they left, I had agreed to deliver their rings to them in Florida, but God had a more providential deliverance in mind.

There was confusion in the airport in Haiti. There was a question as to whether the flight to Florida would happen, since the plane hadn't yet arrived from South America. Finally, the plane did arrive, but when we got to Miami, we discovered that our checked bags had not been loaded on the plane in Port-au-Prince. Several of the Haitian passengers were unable to fill out the baggage claim forms. As I attempted to help them, word spread that I was fluent in Creole, and soon there was a line of people waiting for me to help them. Just as I was starting to feel overwhelmed, an American businessman approached me and asked, "Can I help you?"

I motioned to the line of Haitians awaiting my help to fill out their forms, "Can you write French?"

"Oh yes."

"Fine. You help this lady."

And with that, we worked side-by-side, finished all the forms, and made sure the Haitians had proper understanding and service. I thought that would be the last I would see of the gentleman when I heard him asking me, "What are you doing tonight?"

The airline was taking care of our stay at a hotel for the evening. However, I still needed to travel another thirty to forty-five minutes north to deliver my friends' wedding rings.

The man continued, "I'm renting a car. Maybe I can help you?"

Well, I thought, that is an answer to my need, but I don't want to do anything stupid here. I was very apprehensive of this man. I thought of the rings and money I had buried deep within my clothes and how I didn't want him to take them, or anything else.

On the bus ride over to the hotel, I learned his name was Jacques. We talked more, and I began to gain more confidence in his character. He shared that he, too, was a Christian believer and had a great wife and two teenage children in Connecticut. I eventually accepted his kind offer to drive me to Deerfield Beach.

On the ride north, I learned that Jacques was a widely traveled man. He was fascinated with how I came to be bringing wedding rings to my friends in Deerfield Beach. I explained how Gary and Gail had been impressed at the skill of the goldsmiths working along the road with little more than an acetylene torch, a few obsolete gold coins, and small tongs. They had ordered the final crafted, ornate rings, which I had agreed to make sure they received.

When we arrived at Deerfield Beach, Gary and Gail offered Jacques hospitality, and he offered to drive be back to Miami. On the return trip, Jacques spoke of Wallace and how they had talked at the airport during my departure, unbeknownst to me. When I explained Wallace was my husband, Jacques replied, "Oh, that was your husband." I was so naive; looking back I'm sure he knew who Wallace was and knew more than he told me. He asked many questions about politics, and that's when I told him about Ti Joe.

The Tonton Macouts had brutally massacred two prominent families, killing old and young and burning their houses. Both families were of the long-standing wealthy elite from the colonial days, and one of the grandfathers was a Frenchman. Among the very few who survived the massacre were the three youngest children of the family who had been coming home from school but were stopped by neighbors who hid them until someone could get word to the French Embassy. It was the wife of the French Ambassador who found her way to the Mission on the Kenscoff Road asking if we would take twelve-year-old Georges as she was keeping Gertha and five-year-old Eddy. With three sons of our own, it was easy to have Georges, nicknamed Ti Joe, live quietly at the Mission as the community was used to having white boys around. Wallace and I had discussed ways to get Ti Joe past the Haiti airport checkpoint and boarded on a plane, but that's where our plan ended. We knew there was no possibility of getting him into the United States without a passport.

When I finished my story, Jacques' response was passionate, "We *will* get that boy out of Haiti." Before leaving Miami, he gave me instructions to write a letter to Wallace in code explaining that ere long a he should except to receive sat the Mission the godfather to our "adopted son." I mixed the information in a long letter about the delayed baggage, my visit with Gary and Gail, and sight-seeing in Florida, and mailed it.

All this happened a long time before the TV program *Angels Unaware*, but it was a noteworthy drama and thinking of what Jack accomplished brings it to mind. For Jacques did come to Haiti and the Mission on the Kenscoff Road. In two weeks time, he left with not only Ti Joe, but Gertha and little Eddy as well. The French Ambassador had arranged with the purser on the *SS France* passenger ship for a group of young people from the Mission to get a tour of the ship. The purser knew of the Mission's good reputation and was happy to oblige. A group of foreign mission personnel and our son Sandy, along with his friends, made quite a crew of visitors. Jacques and the three children were among this group. Thankfully, the port immigration had failed to count the number going on the ship or the number coming off!

Three months later, I received a phone call from Jacques. All three children were safe in Connecticut. He was sponsoring Gertha in a private boarding school; Ti Joe and Eddy were traveling to live with their oldest brother who had previously immigrated and was in Maryland. We learned that Ti Joe went on to graduate from George Washington University where he was a champion soccer player and later become a renowned soccer coach.

Wallace and I received a Christmas card from Jacques for many years and would smile when we saw it was signed with the code name "Bill O'Leary." Jacques continued with "non-identified" research for the United States while exploring commercial opportunities for American companies in many parts of the world.

Once when we were in the high mountains of Northern Thailand, a missionary told us the story of his false arrest and imprisonment along with a number of tribal Christians. Government officials had created a scheme for the illegal sale of timber that would only work if those who knew about it— the local Christians and tribesmen—were kept quiet, thus their imprisonment. As the missionary told us of the horror of his imprisonment and the hopelessness of the situation, we became electrified when he mentioned an angel by the name of Jacques who had been sent from God to intervene for them. Here we were in a rather remote area of Thailand, more than 3,000 miles away from Haiti sharing stories about the same Jacques!

Different rumors and theories followed Jacques to his grave. Some said he was CIA, some said a lawyer traveling for big American business firms, while others said he was Secret Service;

his contact and influence with military officials did make one wonder. In our heart of hearts, we knew who Jacques was because we were one of the few who had been touched by an angel. Jacques was a rare, kind, and concerned person ready to embrace other people's problems with relentless tenacity, no matter the costs. He made little proclamation about his deep-rooted Christian faith, but as told in Acts 10:38 of the Master Himself—he went about doing good.

EPILOGUE

When I went to Haiti, the Haitian people became part of my life, but I soon learned that while some people are *in* our lives, others pass *through* our lives. Each one leaves a mark on us, for all of us are intertwined, created for a purpose to do His work.

After almost 70 years of living in Haiti, I have come to believe the story of Haiti's development can be seen in many ways by what happens on the Kenscoff Road and those who travel its bumps and curves. I arrived when the road was but a footpath for women to carry heavy loads of produce from the mountains to the nation's capital, Port-au-Prince. And I was there when the first open-bed truck carried that same produce to the city below. Today, fleets of trucks roar up and down the paved road, passing a seemingly endless view of terraces and green trees to control erosion on the once-bare mountainside. Homes, businesses, schools, and pop-up markets now fill the winding road up and down the mountain.

There were times in those early days when Wallace, my mother, and I felt rather lonely in our house by the side of the road. Even with a deep-seated belief that we were obeying God's call, that He was (and is) ever-present, we couldn't help but wonder—was anybody out there? Did anybody else care about the plight of our neighbors? Today, some have dubbed Haiti the NGO capital of the world, each with a different solution. We could no longer feel alone in our work, even if we tried!

I have also come to see the Kenscoff Road as a metaphor for all the unexpected ways God connects us to one another—a line of grace and faithful provision drawn from one unlikely character to the other, the common goal being His kingdom.

In this book, I have shared but a handful of the stories of those who touched not only my life but also the lives of countless others, sometimes unknowingly. I have laughed and cried while remembering those who passed by the Mission. Each one is special, and I am so thankful to God that they chose to step into the unknown of Haiti to serve. The chain of those who passed by is long; there are so many links—even more than those found in these pages—and God continues to add links every day. Wallace and I are now in our nineties, and we still find ourselves happiest in Haiti on the Kenscoff Road where we continue to welcome those who pass by.

ACKNOWLEDGMENTS

A special thanks to those whose stories have enriched not only my life but also the lives of so many. Their stories are more than could ever be contained in one book.

In nearly a century of living, the memories, names, and events of thousands of people who have passed through my life are bound to get a little mixed up from time to time. For that, I am grateful to my sons Wally and Walter and my daughters-in-law Betty and Mary who helped me unearth the facts and dig deeper when my memory failed me. I give my thanks also to my husband Wallace whose memory astounds me, even in our nineties.

A most special, heartfelt thanks goes to Laura Brown who tackled the daunting task of working closely with me on this book. Her editing has been a great service, and without her help, this collection of stories would have never come to be.

Finally, I extend my thanks to you, dear reader. For in traveling through pages of this book, along the Kenscoff Road, you, too, have become, in a way, one of those who passed by. Your story and mine are now intertwined.

ABOUT THE AUTHOR

E leanor Turnbull has lived and served in Haiti for 70 years with her husband, Wallace, as a pioneer in missions and development. Through her lifetime at the Mission on the Kenscoff Road, Eleanor has cared for hundreds of people who "passed by," many of whom she met through her groundbreaking work in rural medical care.

In spite of having no formal medical training, Eleanor became one of the most respected hospital administrators and medical influencers in the country, working to introduce mobile clinics and family planning in rural communities. She also helped found the nationwide Association of Christian Hospitals, which would establish guidelines and best practices for the major hospitals of other missions across every department of Haiti. For her work and service, Eleanor was decorated as a Grand Officer of the Department of Public Health.

In addition to her medical work, Eleanor was instrumental in introducing child evangelism throughout Haiti. And she helped start some of the first rural Christian primary schools in the country.

Eleanor received her B.A. from Stetson University in 1944 and her M.A. in Biblical Education from Columbia Bible College in 1945. In 2004, she was bestowed an honorary Doctorate of Humanities from Université Jean-Price Mars, and in 2017, she received an honorary Doctorate of Divinity from Liberty University.

Eleanor has three sons (Wallace Jr., Walter, and David), seven grandchildren (Wallace III, Andrew, Ari, Elizabeth, Rodney, Walter, and Nicole), and seven great-grandchildren (Chloe, Gracelyn, Vivian, Skylar, Camden, Stirling, and Lennon).

If you liked

THOSE WHO PASSED BY

you might also enjoy these other titles about Haiti

Say to These Mountains:
A biography of faith and ministry in rural Haiti
Elizabeth Turnbull

God is No Stranger
Sandra Burdick and Eleanor Turnbull

Hidden Meanings: Truth and Secret in Haitian Proverbs
Wally Turnbull

Kite kè m pale (Let My Heart Speak)
Poems in Krèyol
Jacques Pierre

Janjak and Freda Go to the Iron Market
Elizabeth Turnbull

Bonnwit Kabrit (Goodnight Goat)
Elizabeth Turnbull

CPSIA information can be obtained
at www.ICGtesting.com
Printed in the USA
BVOW03s1510010817
490815BV00001B/155/P